The House Flipping Process: A Step-by-Step Guide to Wealth

ALEXANDER MILLER

The House Flipping Process: A Step-by-Step Guide to Wealth

DISCLAIMER

This book is for informational purposes only and does not constitute professional advice. The information contained in this book is not intended to be a substitute for professional advice, including but not limited to real estate, financial, legal, or construction advice. The author and publisher make no representations or warranties of any kind, express or implied, about the completeness, accuracy, reliability, suitability or availability with respect to the book or the information, products, services, or related graphics contained in the book for any purpose. In no event will the author or publisher be liable for any loss or damage including without limitation, indirect or consequential loss or damage, or any loss or damage whatsoever arising from loss of data or profits arising out of, or in connection with, the use of this book.

The opinions expressed in this book are those of the author and do not necessarily reflect the views of the publisher. The author and publisher cannot guarantee the accuracy or completeness of the information and shall not be held liable for any errors or omissions. The information contained in this book is current as of the date of publication, but may be subject to change. The author and publisher make every effort to keep the information up-to-date and correct, but make no representations or warranties of any kind, express or implied, about the completeness, accuracy, reliability, suitability or availability with respect to the book or the information, products, services, or related graphics contained in the book for any purpose.

The House Flipping Process: A Step-by-Step Guide to Wealth

INTRODUCTION

Flipping houses has become a popular investment strategy in the real estate industry. It involves buying a property, renovating it, and then selling it for a profit. The key to success in this business is to find properties that can be purchased at a low cost, to make strategic renovations, and to sell the property at a higher price. This book will guide you through the process of building a successful house flipping business, covering everything from finding properties, to renovating, to marketing and selling. With the right approach and the right team, anyone can build a profitable house flipping business. This book will provide you with the information and tools needed to succeed.

TABLE OF CONTENTS

- Introduction to House Flipping   9

- House Flipping Market Analysis   24

- Finding and Evaluating Properties   41

- Renovation Planning and Management   81

- Marketing and Selling Properties   106

- Building a House Flipping Business   126

- THE END   141

The House Flipping Process: A Step-by-Step Guide to Wealth

Chapter 1

Introduction to House Flipping

House flipping is a popular real estate investment strategy that involves buying, renovating, and selling properties for a profit. This process can be done by individuals or by professional real estate investors who specialize in flipping homes. The goal of house flipping is to buy undervalued properties, make improvements to increase their value, and sell them for a profit.

House flipping can offer a number of benefits, including the potential for significant financial returns, flexible work arrangements, and the opportunity to be creative and hands-on with the renovation process. However, it also requires careful planning, research, and a significant amount of capital to succeed.

Common Misconceptions about House Flipping

There are several misconceptions about house flipping that can deter potential investors. One common myth is that house flipping is easy and requires little effort. In reality, house flipping requires a significant investment of time, energy, and money to research, purchase, and renovate properties.

Another common misconception is that house flipping is a guaranteed way to make money. While there is the potential for significant profits, the success of house flipping is highly dependent on the current real estate market conditions, the condition of the property, and the ability to make improvements that will increase its value.

Types of House Flipping

There are several types of house flipping that investors can pursue, including:

1.   Whole House Renovation: This type of flipping involves purchasing a property that is in poor condition and renovating the entire property to increase its value.

2.   Cosmetics-Only Renovation: This type of flipping involves making minor cosmetic improvements to a property, such as painting, new fixtures, or landscaping, to increase its value.

3.   Wholesale Flipping: This type of flipping involves buying a property below market value, making minimal improvements, and selling it to another investor for a profit.

Setting Your House Flipping Goals

The House Flipping Process: A Step-by-Step Guide to Wealth

Before beginning the house flipping process, it is important to set specific, achievable goals. These goals should take into account your financial situation, experience, and personal preferences. Some common house flipping goals include:

1. Financial Goals: Determine the amount of money you want to make from each flip and how many flips you want to complete per year.

2. Timeframe Goals: Set a deadline for completing each flip, taking into account the time required for research, renovation, and sales.

3. Personal Goals: Consider your personal interests, skills, and preferences for the type of properties you want to flip, such as location, property type, and renovation style.

By setting clear and achievable house flipping goals, you can focus your efforts and increase your chances of success.

In addition to setting goals, it is also important to have a solid understanding of the real estate market and the house flipping process. This includes researching market trends, learning about the renovation process and building codes, and developing a network of real estate professionals, such as real estate agents, inspectors, and contractors.

Before making a purchase, it is important to conduct a thorough analysis of the property and its potential for profit. This includes reviewing the property's value, condition, and potential return on investment (ROI), as well as any potential risks or challenges that may arise during the renovation process.

Finally, it is essential to have a solid financial plan in place before beginning the house flipping process. This includes securing financing, setting a budget, and establishing a contingency plan in case of unexpected expenses or market changes.

In conclusion, house flipping can be a highly rewarding and profitable investment strategy, but it requires careful planning, research, and preparation to succeed. By setting clear goals, conducting thorough market analysis, and having a solid financial plan in place, you can increase your chances of success and build a successful house flipping business.

It is also important to have a strong understanding of the real estate laws and regulations in your area. This includes obtaining any necessary permits, complying with building codes and zoning laws, and understanding the tax implications of your investments.

Additionally, it is important to have a solid marketing plan in place to help you successfully sell your renovated properties. This includes developing a professional and appealing listing, utilizing a variety of marketing channels to reach potential buyers, and working with a real estate agent to negotiate the best deal for you.

Another key component of house flipping success is effective project management. This includes creating a detailed project plan, selecting the right contractors and suppliers, and overseeing the renovation process to ensure that the work is completed on time and within budget.

Finally, it is important to continuously educate yourself and stay up-to-date on the latest house flipping techniques and strategies. This includes attending workshops and seminars, reading industry publications, and networking with other experienced house flippers.

In summary, the house flipping process involves a number of important steps, including setting goals, conducting market research, securing financing, understanding real estate laws and regulations, having a solid marketing plan, effective project management, and continuous education. By following these steps, you can increase your chances of success and achieve your financial and personal goals as a house flipper.

It is also advisable to have a solid team in place to help you with the house flipping process. This includes a real estate agent, a contractor, an inspector, and a financial advisor. These professionals can provide valuable advice, support, and guidance throughout the process, helping to minimize potential risks and ensure a successful outcome.

It is important to remember that house flipping is not a get-rich-quick scheme, and success requires hard work, patience, and persistence. While there may be some bumps along the way, the rewards of successful house flipping can be substantial, including increased wealth, financial stability, and personal satisfaction.

Another aspect to consider is the cost of the renovations. This includes the cost of materials, labor, and any necessary upgrades, such as electrical, plumbing, or HVAC systems. To maximize profits, it is important to keep renovation costs under control while still maintaining the quality and value of the property.

Finally, it is important to have a clear exit strategy in place, including how and when you will sell the property. This can involve a direct sale to a buyer or a more complex strategy, such as leveraging the property for future investments.

In conclusion, house flipping is a complex and challenging process, but with the right approach, it can also be highly rewarding. By setting clear goals, conducting thorough research, having a solid financial plan, and building a strong team, you can increase your chances of success and achieve your financial and personal goals as a house flipper.

When it comes to the actual renovation process, there are several key considerations to keep in mind. One of the most important is ensuring that the work is done to the highest standards, while also keeping safety in mind. This means selecting the right contractors, obtaining necessary permits, and adhering to building codes and safety regulations.

Another key consideration is timing. It is important to have a realistic timeline for the renovation process and to account for any potential delays or obstacles that may arise.

This can include unexpected repair costs, weather conditions, or delays in obtaining necessary permits.

Another key component of the renovation process is budget management. This includes monitoring expenses, controlling costs, and making sure that the project stays within budget. To help with this, it is advisable to have a detailed project budget in place and to regularly track and update it throughout the renovation process.

It is also important to have a clear and effective communication plan in place with all stakeholders involved in the project, including contractors, real estate agents, and inspectors. This helps to ensure that everyone is on the same page, that the project stays on track, and that any issues are addressed in a timely and effective manner.

Finally, it is important to have a contingency plan in place in case of any unexpected events or issues that may arise during the renovation process. This can include unexpected repair costs, market changes, or other factors that may impact the success of the project.

In summary, the renovation process is a critical component of the house flipping process, and requires careful planning, budget management, effective communication, and contingency planning to ensure success. By following these steps, you can ensure that your renovations are completed on time, within budget, and to the highest standards, helping to maximize profits and achieve your financial goals.

The House Flipping Process: A Step-by-Step Guide to Wealth

In addition to the renovation process, there are several other key steps that are involved in house flipping. One of the most important is conducting thorough research and due diligence. This includes analyzing market trends, researching property values and sales prices, and identifying target neighborhoods or areas. It is also important to consider factors such as the local economy, infrastructure, and population demographics, as these can all have a significant impact on the success of the project.

Another important step is to have a solid financial plan in place. This includes obtaining financing for the project, whether through a loan, line of credit, or other financing options. It is also important to have a clear understanding of the costs involved, including acquisition costs, renovation costs, and holding costs, such as property taxes, insurance, and utilities.

Once the renovation process is complete, it is time to market the property. This can involve staging the property, creating an effective marketing strategy, and pricing the property competitively to attract potential buyers. It is also important to consider the target market, such as first-time homebuyers, families, or retirees, and to tailor the marketing approach accordingly.

When it comes time to sell the property, it is important to work with a real estate agent who has experience in the local market and can assist with negotiations, marketing, and closing the sale. It is also important to have a clear understanding of the closing process, including any necessary documentation, transfer of ownership, and disbursement of funds.

Finally, it is important to review and evaluate the success of the project, and to use this information to refine and improve future house flipping ventures. This includes analyzing the financial performance of the project, tracking expenses and profits, and reviewing lessons learned for future reference.

In conclusion, house flipping involves a series of steps, each of which is critical to the success of the project. By conducting thorough research and due diligence, having a solid financial plan, marketing the property effectively, working with a real estate agent, and reviewing and evaluating the project, you can increase your chances of success and achieve your financial goals as a house flipper.

It is important to remember that house flipping is not a passive investment, but rather a hands-on, actively managed process. This requires a significant amount of time, effort, and commitment, and it is not suitable for everyone. Before embarking on a house flipping venture, it is important to consider your personal skills, experience, and financial situation.

House flipping can be a challenging and demanding process, and it is important to be well prepared and organized. This includes having a clear understanding of the local real estate market, knowing the key players in the market, and being able to identify potential properties that meet your investment criteria.

Additionally, it is important to have a clear and concise business plan in place, outlining your investment strategy, timeline, budget, and goals. This helps to keep you focused and on track, and provides a roadmap for success.

One of the keys to success in house flipping is to have a thorough understanding of the renovation process and the various steps involved. This includes selecting the right contractors, obtaining necessary permits, adhering to building codes and safety regulations, managing expenses, and ensuring that the project stays on schedule.

Another critical factor is having access to the right resources and tools, including real estate software, market data and analysis, and professional connections. This helps to streamline the process, reduce costs, and increase your chances of success.

Finally, it is important to remain flexible and adaptable, and to be willing to pivot or make changes as needed. The real estate market is constantly changing, and it is important to be able to adapt to market conditions and capitalize on new opportunities as they arise.

In conclusion, house flipping is a complex and challenging process that requires a significant amount of preparation, effort, and commitment. However, for those who are well prepared and have the right skills and experience, it can be a lucrative and rewarding venture, offering the potential for significant financial returns and a path to financial independence.

When it comes to house flipping, having a solid understanding of the local real estate market is essential. This includes knowledge of current market trends, property values, and local zoning regulations, as well as a deep understanding of the buying and selling process. This information can help you identify properties that have the greatest potential for profit and help you make informed decisions about which properties to pursue.

Another key aspect of successful house flipping is having access to the right financing. Whether you are using your own funds, seeking private funding, or obtaining a loan from a financial institution, it is important to have the necessary resources to finance the purchase and renovation of your property.

One of the biggest challenges in house flipping is managing the renovation process. This includes working with contractors, overseeing the work being done, and ensuring that the project stays on schedule and within budget. It is important to have a solid understanding of the construction process, as well as good communication skills, so that you can work effectively with your contractors and keep the project on track.

In addition to the renovation process, it is also important to be able to effectively market and sell the property once the renovation is complete. This includes having a strong understanding of the real estate sales process, as well as marketing and advertising skills, so that you can effectively showcase the property and attract potential buyers.

Finally, it is important to have a well-defined exit strategy in place. This includes having a clear understanding of your goals, timeline, and budget, as well as a plan for how you will sell the property once the renovation is complete. Whether you are planning to sell the property for a profit, rent it out, or use it as a primary residence, having a clear and concise exit strategy can help to ensure that your house flipping venture is a success.

In conclusion, house flipping is a complex and demanding process that requires a significant amount of preparation, effort, and commitment. However, for those who are well prepared and have the right skills and experience, it can be a lucrative and rewarding venture, offering the potential for significant financial returns and a path to financial independence.

As a house flipper, it is important to have a network of professionals who can support you along the way. This includes a real estate agent who understands the local market, a trustworthy and experienced contractor, an inspector to assess the condition of the property, and a reliable and knowledgeable accountant to help you manage your finances. Building strong relationships with these professionals can help to ensure that the house flipping process goes smoothly and that you have the resources you need to be successful.

One important consideration when flipping a house is the budget. It is crucial to have a clear understanding of the cost of the renovation, as well as the potential resale value of the property. This will help you determine how much you can afford to spend, how much you will need to borrow, and what your potential return on investment will be. It is also important to have a contingency plan in place in case unexpected costs arise during the renovation process.

Another key factor to consider when flipping a house is the timeline. It is important to have a realistic understanding of how long it will take to complete the renovation and how long it will take to sell the property once it is complete. This will help you determine when you will have a return on your investment and when you can start to see a profit.

It is also important to understand the risks involved in house flipping. This includes the potential for market fluctuations, changes in zoning regulations, and the possibility of hidden damages or problems with the property. It is important to carefully assess the risks and to have a plan in place to mitigate them.

In summary, house flipping can be a challenging and rewarding venture, but it requires careful planning, preparation, and attention to detail. By understanding the local real estate market, having access to the right financing and professional support, managing the renovation process effectively, and having a clear and concise exit strategy, you can maximize your chances of success and achieve your financial goals.

The first step in the house flipping process is to find the right property. This involves conducting market research to understand the local real estate market, identifying properties that have the potential for renovation and resale, and evaluating the financial viability of the project. One important consideration when searching for a property is location. Properties that are located in desirable neighborhoods or close to amenities are likely to be in high demand and command higher prices.

Once you have found a potential property, it is important to conduct a thorough inspection. This involves hiring a professional inspector who can assess the condition of the property and identify any potential problems or repairs that may be needed. The inspector will also provide you with a report that outlines the findings and provides recommendations for repairs and upgrades. This information will help you determine whether the property is a good investment opportunity and will inform your renovation and budgeting decisions.

Another key aspect of the house flipping process is the renovation. This involves making necessary repairs and upgrades to the property in order to increase its value and appeal to potential buyers. This may involve updating the kitchen and bathrooms, repainting the interior and exterior of the property, and making any necessary repairs to the roof, plumbing, or electrical systems. It is important to have a clear understanding of the scope of the renovation and to plan accordingly, taking into account the budget and timeline.

The final step in the house flipping process is the sale. This involves marketing the property to potential buyers and negotiating the sale price. It is important to have a clear understanding of the target market for the property and to make the necessary updates and upgrades to appeal to that market. It is also important to price the property appropriately, taking into account the value of similar properties in the area and the cost of the renovation.

House flipping is a complex process that requires careful planning, attention to detail, and an understanding of the real estate market. By taking the time to research the market, identify the right property, conduct a thorough inspection, and plan the renovation effectively, you can maximize your chances of success and achieve your financial goals.

In conclusion, the Introduction to House Flipping lays the foundation for the rest of the book and provides an overview of the key steps involved in the process. Understanding the basics of house flipping is essential for anyone who wants to start investing in real estate and building wealth through property renovation and resale. As you read through the subsequent chapters, you will gain a deeper understanding of the various aspects of house flipping and will be equipped with the knowledge and skills you need to succeed in this exciting and rewarding investment opportunity.

"Real estate investing, especially house flipping, is not just about making a profit, it's about creating a legacy."

Chapter 2

House Flipping Market Analysis

In order to succeed in the world of house flipping, it is crucial to have a deep understanding of the local real estate market. This chapter focuses on how to analyze the market to identify the best investment opportunities and maximize your chances of success.

One of the first steps in market analysis is to research the local housing market. This involves studying the trends in property values, rental prices, and sales volume, as well as demographic and economic factors that may impact the market. By understanding the current market conditions, you can determine whether it is a good time to invest in real estate and identify the types of properties that are in high demand.

Another important aspect of market analysis is to research the competition. This involves studying the other investors and developers who are active in the market and evaluating their strategies and success rates. By understanding what other investors are doing and what types of properties are selling well, you can refine your own investment strategy and identify areas where you can differentiate yourself from the competition.

It is also important to research the local zoning and building regulations, as these can have a significant impact on the feasibility and profitability of a house flipping project. For example, zoning regulations may determine whether you are able to add additional square footage to the property or construct a separate unit on the property. Building regulations may also impact the cost and timeline of the renovation, so it is important to understand these regulations before you begin your project.

In conclusion, market analysis is a critical aspect of the house flipping process. By conducting a thorough analysis of the local real estate market, you can identify the best investment opportunities, understand the competition, and navigate the regulatory environment. This information will help you make informed decisions about your investment strategy and increase your chances of success.

Additionally, when conducting a market analysis, it is important to consider the potential return on investment (ROI) of a property. This involves calculating the expected profit from the sale of the property, taking into account the cost of the renovation, real estate taxes, closing costs, and any other expenses that may be associated with the project. By evaluating the potential ROI of each property, you can compare the different investment opportunities available to you and choose the ones that offer the best potential for profit.

It is also essential to consider the target market for the properties you are flipping. Understanding the demographic and lifestyle characteristics of the people who are likely to buy or rent the property can help you make informed decisions about the design, features, and finishes that will appeal to them. For example, if you are flipping a property in a neighborhood that is popular with young families, you may want to consider adding features like a playroom or a spacious backyard. On the other hand, if you are flipping a property in a neighborhood that is popular with empty nesters, you may want to focus on creating a more low-maintenance living space with upscale finishes.

Another important aspect of market analysis is to identify the potential risks associated with a property. This may include factors such as the age of the property, the condition of the roof, the presence of any environmental hazards, and any other issues that may impact the value of the property. By considering these risks and developing a plan to mitigate them, you can reduce your exposure to risk and increase your chances of success.

In conclusion, conducting a thorough market analysis is a crucial step in the house flipping process. By considering the factors described above, you can identify the best investment opportunities, evaluate the potential ROI of each property, understand your target market, and reduce your exposure to risk. These insights will help you make informed decisions and increase your chances of success.

It is also important to stay up-to-date with the latest market trends and changes in real estate regulations. Regularly reading industry news and attending relevant events or workshops can help you stay informed and make informed decisions. Additionally, working with a real estate agent or market analyst who has experience and expertise in your target market can also be extremely helpful. These professionals can provide you with valuable insights, advice, and resources that can help you make the most of your investment.

It is also important to consider the overall health of the housing market. Factors such as unemployment rates, interest rates, and economic conditions can impact the demand for housing and influence the prices of properties. By keeping an eye on these trends and adjusting your strategy accordingly, you can minimize your risk and capitalize on the best opportunities.

Finally, it is crucial to remember that the success of your house flipping project depends on your ability to effectively manage the entire process. This includes not just the market analysis but also the acquisition, renovation, and sale of the property. By developing a clear plan and strategy, setting realistic goals, and staying organized and focused, you can increase your chances of success and achieve your financial goals.

In conclusion, market analysis is a critical component of the house flipping process that should not be overlooked. By staying informed, working with experienced professionals, considering market trends and conditions, and managing the process effectively, you can increase your chances of success and achieve your financial goals.

Additionally, it is important to understand the supply and demand dynamics in your target market. You should research the number of properties for sale and the number of potential buyers in the area to determine the level of competition you will face. If there are more properties available than there are buyers, it may be more difficult to sell your flipped property at a profit. On the other hand, if there is high demand for housing and low supply, you may be able to sell your property more quickly and at a higher price.

It is also important to consider the demographics of the area you are targeting. Understanding the age, income, and education levels of potential buyers can help you make informed decisions about the type of properties to flip, the renovation and design elements to incorporate, and the marketing strategies to use. For example, if your target market is young professionals, you may want to focus on properties with modern finishes and convenient locations near public transportation and entertainment options.

Another key aspect of market analysis is determining the price range for similar properties in the area. This will give you an idea of how much you can spend on the acquisition and renovation of the property, as well as the potential profit you can make from the sale. It is important to research recent sales data for comparable properties in the area to get an accurate picture of the current market conditions. You can also use online tools and resources to estimate the value of the property before and after the renovations.

In summary, market analysis is a critical step in the house flipping process that requires careful research and planning. By considering factors such as supply and demand, demographics, and pricing, you can make informed decisions and maximize your chances of success.

Additionally, it is important to stay informed about local real estate trends and regulations that may affect your ability to flip properties. For example, you may need to be aware of zoning laws, building codes, and environmental regulations that could impact the feasibility and profitability of your project. Keeping up with local news and market reports can help you stay ahead of the curve and make informed decisions.

Another aspect to consider is the current state of the economy and how it may impact the housing market. For example, during a recession, people may be less likely to buy homes, making it more difficult to sell your flipped property at a profit. On the other hand, during a period of economic growth, there may be more demand for housing and higher prices, making it easier to make money from flipping properties.

Finally, it is important to assess the competition in your market. Who are your competitors and what are they doing to stay ahead in the market? By understanding their strengths and weaknesses, you can identify areas where you can differentiate yourself and offer a unique value proposition to potential buyers. This can help you stand out in a crowded market and attract more buyers to your properties.

In conclusion, market analysis is an ongoing process that requires constant attention and adaptation. By staying informed and proactive, you can make smart decisions, overcome challenges, and achieve success in your house flipping business.

It is also advisable to study the demographics of the areas where you are considering flipping houses. This can give you insights into the type of people who are likely to buy your properties, including their age, income, and family size. For example, if the area has a high population of young families, you may want to focus on flipping properties that are family-friendly and have features such as large yards, playgrounds, and good schools.

Additionally, you should consider the local employment market when assessing a potential flipping market. Areas with high employment and job growth tend to have a strong demand for housing and could provide you with more opportunities for profit. On the other hand, areas with high unemployment rates may struggle to attract buyers, making it more difficult to flip properties for a profit.

It is also important to be aware of the current state of the housing market in the areas where you are considering flipping properties. For example, if there is a surplus of housing, it may be more challenging to sell your flipped property at a profit. On the other hand, if there is a high demand for housing and a shortage of available properties, you may be able to sell your property quickly and at a higher price.

In summary, house flipping market analysis requires you to be well-informed and up-to-date with the latest market trends and conditions. By taking the time to research and analyze your market, you can make smart decisions and increase your chances of success in the house flipping business.

It is also important to have a good understanding of the local real estate laws and regulations. This includes knowing the zoning laws, building codes, and any restrictions that may affect your ability to flip properties. Failure to comply with these laws can result in costly fines, penalties, and even legal proceedings, which can negatively impact your profits.

Another factor to consider when conducting house flipping market analysis is the competition. Research your competitors to determine what they are doing, their strengths, and weaknesses. This information can help you to identify areas where you can differentiate yourself from your competition and offer unique value to potential buyers.

Finally, it is important to have a clear understanding of your target market when conducting house flipping market analysis. This includes identifying the type of properties that your target market is interested in and the specific features that they value. By knowing what your target market is looking for, you can make smart decisions when it comes to flipping properties that are likely to be in high demand.

In conclusion, the house flipping market analysis is a crucial step in the house flipping process. By taking the time to thoroughly research and analyze your market, you can increase your chances of success and avoid costly mistakes. By staying informed, understanding the competition, and knowing your target market, you can make smart decisions and achieve your goal of generating wealth through house flipping.

It is also recommended to keep an eye on real estate trends and market indicators, such as average home prices, home sales, and rental prices, to gauge the overall health of the real estate market. Understanding these trends can help you to identify areas that may be ripe for flipping, as well as identify areas where you may need to exercise caution.

Additionally, it is important to consider the economic conditions of the area when conducting house flipping market analysis. This includes factors such as employment rates, population growth, and economic development. These factors can all impact the demand for housing, which in turn can impact the profitability of your flipping efforts.

Finally, it is important to have a clear understanding of your personal goals and financial resources when conducting house flipping market analysis. This includes determining the amount of money you have available to invest, as well as the level of risk you are comfortable with. By having a clear understanding of your goals and resources, you can make informed decisions when it comes to choosing the right properties to flip.

In conclusion, the house flipping market analysis is an essential part of the house flipping process that requires careful consideration and research. By conducting a thorough market analysis, you can make informed decisions that increase your chances of success and minimize your risk. By staying informed, understanding your goals, and considering all relevant factors, you can make smart decisions that help you achieve your goal of generating wealth through house flipping.

It's also a good idea to take the time to learn about the local zoning laws and regulations, as well as any environmental or historical restrictions that may impact your ability to make changes to the property. This information can be obtained by contacting the local government or a real estate attorney.

It's important to research the crime rates of the area you're considering flipping in as well. High crime rates can make it difficult to sell a property, and may also affect the resale value of the property. By researching crime statistics, you can get a better sense of the safety and security of the neighborhood and make a more informed decision about whether or not to invest in the area.

Furthermore, you should also take the time to research the local schools, shops, and other amenities. Properties located in areas with good schools and a variety of amenities tend to have a higher resale value and are more likely to attract potential buyers.

The House Flipping Process: A Step-by-Step Guide to Wealth

In addition to researching the local market, it's also a good idea to research the types of properties you're interested in flipping. This may include single-family homes, duplexes, triplexes, or apartment buildings. Understanding the different types of properties available, as well as the associated risks and rewards, can help you make a more informed decision when choosing properties to flip.

Overall, conducting a thorough market analysis is a critical step in the house flipping process. By researching the local market, understanding the types of properties available, and considering all relevant factors, you can increase your chances of success and minimize your risk.

Another important factor to consider when conducting market analysis is the current real estate market conditions. This includes analyzing market trends, such as the average sales price of homes in the area, the average days on market, and the number of homes currently for sale. This information can be obtained from real estate websites, real estate agents, or by reviewing public records.

Additionally, it's important to keep an eye on the local economy and job market. A strong local economy with a high demand for housing can result in higher home values and faster sales, making it a more attractive market for flipping. On the other hand, if the local economy is struggling, it may take longer to sell a property and you may face competition from other flippers looking to sell in a buyer's market.

The House Flipping Process: A Step-by-Step Guide to Wealth

Finally, it's also important to research the competition in the area. This includes understanding the types of properties being flipped and the average profit margins. By understanding the competition, you can make sure your property stands out and you can also adjust your strategy accordingly to maximize your profit potential.

In conclusion, conducting a thorough market analysis is a crucial step in the house flipping process. By researching the local market conditions, understanding the competition, and considering all relevant factors, you can make a well-informed decision about where to invest and how to maximize your profits.

Another aspect of market analysis is to identify the target market for the flipped property. This includes understanding the demographics of the area, such as the average household income, age range, and family size, as well as the types of amenities and services that are in demand. For example, if the area is popular with young families, then you may want to consider adding extra bedrooms or a backyard to the property to make it more attractive to that demographic.

It's also important to research the local zoning regulations and building codes. This includes understanding the maximum height of buildings, the required setbacks from the property line, and any restrictions on the type of construction that can be done. This information can help you determine if a property is worth flipping or if there are too many limitations in place.

The House Flipping Process: A Step-by-Step Guide to Wealth

In addition, you should also research the local real estate market to determine the average sales price of similar properties in the area. This information can help you determine the potential profit margins for flipping the property and what kind of renovations or upgrades will be necessary to make the property more marketable.

Finally, it's important to consider the location of the property when conducting market analysis. Properties in highly desirable areas, such as those close to popular attractions or with good access to public transportation, are more likely to be in demand and sell quickly. On the other hand, properties located in areas with higher crime rates or lower property values may take longer to sell and may not be worth flipping.

In conclusion, conducting a thorough market analysis is an important step in the house flipping process. By researching the local real estate market, understanding the target market and competition, and considering all relevant factors, you can make an informed decision about where and how to invest in the market.

Another key aspect of market analysis is to monitor the real estate market trends. This includes paying attention to factors such as rising or falling home prices, changes in interest rates, and any shifts in consumer behavior or market demand. By staying informed about market trends, you can better predict future market conditions and adjust your investment strategy accordingly.

Additionally, it's important to keep track of economic indicators such as inflation, unemployment rates, and consumer confidence, as these can also impact the real estate market. For example, a declining economy could lead to lower consumer confidence, which could in turn impact the demand for housing.

It's also wise to conduct a competitive analysis to understand the other players in the market. This includes researching other flippers in the area, their strategies and successes, and the types of properties they are flipping. By understanding the competition, you can differentiate your approach and position yourself in a way that sets you apart from the rest.

Finally, it's important to consider the timing of your investment. For example, if the local market is experiencing a period of growth, it may be a good time to invest in a property, as prices are likely to continue to rise. On the other hand, if the market is flat or declining, it may be wise to wait for conditions to improve before making an investment.

In conclusion, market analysis is a crucial aspect of the house flipping process, as it provides valuable information about the local real estate market, competition, and market trends. By conducting a thorough analysis and considering all relevant factors, you can make informed decisions about where and when to invest, and maximize your potential for success.

It's also important to conduct a local market analysis to identify the areas with the highest potential for profit. Factors to consider include the average home price, rental rates, and the number of homes for sale in the area. A neighborhood with a high demand for rental properties and a low supply of homes for sale may be a good option for flipping.

Another factor to consider is the type of property that you want to flip. For example, single-family homes are often a popular option, but you may also consider flipping condos or townhouses, or investing in multi-unit properties. Consider factors such as the cost of renovation, the estimated resale value, and the potential rental income when making your decision.

Finally, it's important to consider the timing of your market analysis. For example, if the local real estate market is experiencing a period of growth, it may be a good time to invest in a property. On the other hand, if the market is declining, it may be wise to wait for conditions to improve before making an investment.

In conclusion, a well-conducted market analysis is essential for success in house flipping. By considering factors such as local market trends, competition, and the timing of your investment, you can make informed decisions about where and when to invest, and maximize your potential for profit.

Additionally, researching and understanding the local zoning laws and regulations can be helpful in finding the right properties to flip. Make sure to take into account any restrictions on the property such as building height limits, lot size, and parking requirements. These regulations can affect the value and usability of a property, and may impact your ability to flip it for a profit.

Moreover, it's important to consider the current state of the economy and its effect on the real estate market. For example, if interest rates are low, people are more likely to purchase homes, increasing the demand for homes. On the other hand, if interest rates are high, people may be more hesitant to buy, decreasing the demand for homes. Understanding the current economic trends and their impact on the real estate market can help you make more informed decisions when flipping homes.

Finally, it's important to stay up-to-date with industry trends and news. Reading real estate blogs, attending local real estate events, and networking with other real estate professionals can provide you with valuable information and insights that can help you succeed in house flipping.

By conducting a thorough market analysis, you can gain a better understanding of the local real estate market and make more informed decisions when flipping homes. With the right research and preparation, you can maximize your chances of success and achieve your financial goals through house flipping.

In conclusion, conducting a thorough market analysis is a critical step in the house flipping process. By taking the time to understand the local real estate market, researching local zoning laws and regulations, considering the state of the economy, and staying up-to-date with industry trends, you can position yourself for success and achieve your financial goals through house flipping. A well-executed market analysis sets the foundation for the rest of the house flipping process, so make sure to give it the time and attention it deserves.

"Successful house flipping begins with understanding the market and anticipating its needs."

Chapter 3

Finding and Evaluating Properties

Finding the right property to flip is crucial to the success of your house flipping venture. In this chapter, we will delve into the process of finding and evaluating properties to ensure that you make informed and profitable decisions.

- **Defining Your Target Market:**

Before you begin your search for properties, it's essential to have a clear understanding of the target market you want to serve. Consider factors such as location, property type, target demographic, and budget. This will help you narrow down your search and focus on properties that meet your criteria.

- **Property Sources:**

There are numerous sources for finding potential properties, including real estate listings, auction sites, MLS (Multiple Listing Service), and real estate agents. Utilize a combination of sources to ensure you're getting the most comprehensive list of properties available.

- **Property Evaluation:**

Once you have a list of potential properties, it's time to evaluate them. Start by reviewing the property's condition, including the structural integrity and any necessary repairs or renovations. Next, consider factors such as the property's location, the surrounding neighborhood, and its resale value.

- **Using Technology:**

In today's digital age, there are several tools and technology options available to aid in the property evaluation process. Consider using online tools such as property data sites and home renovation cost calculators to help you make informed decisions.

- **Hiring a Professional Inspector:**

Hiring a professional inspector to perform a thorough inspection of the property can help identify any potential issues that may not be visible to the untrained eye. The inspector's report will give you an in-depth understanding of the property's condition and help you make an informed decision about whether or not to move forward with the purchase.

- **Negotiating the Purchase Price:**

Once you've completed the evaluation process and have decided to move forward with a property, it's time to negotiate the purchase price. Be sure to take into account any necessary repairs and renovations, as well as your desired profit margin, when negotiating the price.

One of the key components of house flipping is finding the right properties to invest in. There are a variety of strategies that you can use to locate properties that have potential for profit. Some popular strategies include:

1. **Driving for dollars:** This involves driving through neighborhoods and looking for properties that appear to be in need of repair or have been neglected. These properties can often be purchased for a low price and then renovated for a profit.

2. **Online property listings:** There are many websites that specialize in real estate listings, and these can be a great source of potential properties. You can use filters to search for properties in your target area, price range, and with specific features you are looking for.

3. **Networking:** Building a network of real estate agents, contractors, and other professionals in the industry can help you locate properties that may not be publicly listed. These individuals often have access to off-market properties that can be a great investment opportunity.

Once you have located potential properties, the next step is to evaluate them. This involves determining whether the property has the potential to generate a profit. Some factors to consider when evaluating properties include:

1. Location: The location of the property will play a major role in its resale value. Properties in areas with good schools, low crime rates, and amenities such as shopping and dining will typically command a higher price.

2. Repair costs: You will need to have a clear understanding of the costs involved in repairing and renovating the property. This will help you determine whether the potential profit from the sale is worth the investment.

3. Resale value: Estimating the resale value of the property after repairs and renovations will help you determine your potential profit margin. This can be done using online real estate tools, or by consulting with a real estate agent.

With these strategies and evaluations in mind, you will be able to find and evaluate properties with the potential for a successful flip.

When it comes to house flipping, finding the right property is the first and most critical step. It's important to locate a property that has good potential for profit and has the right features for a quick and successful flip. In this chapter, we'll discuss how to find and evaluate properties that meet these criteria.

One of the most straightforward ways to find properties is to look at local listings. You can do this online or through a real estate agent. Real estate agents have access to a vast database of properties, so they can provide you with a list of properties that fit your criteria. You can also look for properties that are up for auction, or you can search for properties that are being sold by the owner, also known as a For Sale by Owner (FSBO).

When evaluating properties, it's crucial to keep in mind the three most important factors: location, condition, and value. Location refers to the area in which the property is located and its proximity to amenities like schools, hospitals, shopping centers, and transportation. The condition of the property refers to the state of repair and the amount of work needed to make it livable. Finally, value refers to the price of the property in comparison to its market value.

To get a good understanding of a property's value, you can conduct a property market analysis. This analysis involves looking at the prices of comparable properties in the area and estimating the property's worth. You can also use online tools like Zillow and Redfin to determine a property's estimated value.

Once you've evaluated a property and determined that it meets your criteria, you'll need to make an offer. When making an offer, it's important to keep in mind that the price should be in line with the market value and also account for the cost of repairs.

In conclusion, finding and evaluating properties is an important step in the house flipping process. By considering location, condition, and value, you can identify properties that have good potential for profit and make an informed decision when making an offer.

In finding and evaluating properties, it is important to keep in mind your target market and their needs. Look for properties in areas with strong demand and good potential for growth. Additionally, consider the condition of the property and the cost of any necessary renovations. A good evaluation should also include a thorough inspection of the property to identify any potential issues that may affect its value.

Another important aspect to consider is the property's location. A property located in a good neighborhood with good schools, safe streets and proximity to shopping, dining and other amenities will have a higher value. On the other hand, a property located in a declining neighborhood or an area with high crime rates may be less appealing to potential buyers.

Finally, research the current real estate market conditions in the area. Look for trends and patterns that may indicate whether the market is going up or down. This will help you make informed decisions about which properties to invest in.

In conclusion, finding and evaluating properties requires careful research, attention to detail, and a clear understanding of your target market and the real estate market conditions. By doing this, you can find properties that are a good investment, with high potential for profit.

Another important aspect to consider when finding and evaluating properties is the property's financials. This includes the purchase price, the cost of any renovations, and the potential sales price. Make sure to carefully consider the costs involved and whether the property will provide a positive return on investment (ROI).

Additionally, you may want to consider hiring a professional inspector to give you a detailed evaluation of the property. An inspector will be able to identify any major issues with the property that may affect its value and make recommendations for repairs or renovations.

It is also important to consider the competition in the area. Research other similar properties in the area to see what they are selling for and what features they have that may make them appealing to potential buyers. This will help you determine the potential sales price of your property and whether it will be a good investment.

In addition to the physical and financial aspects of a property, it is important to also consider the legal and regulatory aspects. Make sure to research any zoning laws, building codes, and any other regulations that may affect the property. This will help you avoid any legal issues down the road and ensure that the property is in compliance with all regulations.

Finally, when evaluating properties, it is important to have a clear understanding of your goals and the goals of your target market. This will help you make informed decisions about which properties to invest in and how to market them to potential buyers.

When evaluating properties, it's important to consider factors such as location, market conditions, and the condition of the property itself. Location is key, as certain areas may be in high demand, while others may be declining. It's also important to consider the surrounding neighborhood and any nearby amenities, such as schools, parks, and shopping centers.

The condition of the property should also be closely examined. This includes evaluating the structure of the building, as well as its mechanical systems, such as plumbing, electrical, and heating. A thorough inspection should be performed by a professional, as hidden issues can impact the overall value of the property.

Another important factor to consider is the market conditions. This involves researching current real estate trends, as well as considering factors such as the unemployment rate, local economy, and interest rates. Understanding the market can help you make informed decisions about buying and flipping properties.

Ultimately, finding and evaluating properties requires a combination of research, intuition, and experience. It's important to take your time and not rush into any decisions, as this can lead to costly mistakes. By taking a systematic approach, you can increase your chances of success in the house flipping business.

When it comes to finding and evaluating properties, it is important to have a clear strategy in place. One way to approach this is by using a combination of online and offline resources, such as real estate websites, MLS listings, local newspapers, and word-of-mouth referrals.

Another important factor to consider is location, as the location of the property will have a significant impact on its potential for appreciation and resale value. This means researching demographic data, crime rates, and other factors that may affect the desirability of the neighborhood.

Once you have identified potential properties, it is important to perform a thorough evaluation of each property to determine its potential for renovation and resale. This should include a physical inspection of the property, as well as an evaluation of the surrounding neighborhood and local real estate market.

In addition to the physical inspection, it is important to also obtain a professional home inspection report, which can provide valuable insights into any potential issues with the property such as structural damage, electrical or plumbing problems, and other critical factors.

Finally, it is important to consider the costs associated with the renovation and resale of the property, including the cost of materials, labor, and any necessary permits or fees. This information will be critical in determining the feasibility of the project, and can help you make an informed decision on whether to move forward with the purchase.

Overall, finding and evaluating properties requires a strategic and methodical approach, as well as a thorough understanding of the local real estate market and the costs associated with the renovation and resale of properties.

When evaluating properties, it is important to look at both the interior and exterior of the property. Take into consideration the condition of the roof, windows, doors, and any other structural elements. Evaluate the plumbing and electrical systems to ensure that they are up-to-date and functional. Look for any signs of damage or wear and tear, such as water damage, cracks in the walls or foundation, or outdated appliances.

Consider the location of the property, including the neighborhood and nearby amenities, such as parks, schools, shopping centers, and public transportation. A property in a desirable area with access to these amenities is likely to have higher resale value.

It is also important to do your research and check property records, including the sale history and current ownership, to make sure you are fully informed about the property you are interested in. This information can help you determine whether a property is a good investment, and whether there are any potential roadblocks that could impact your profits.

Lastly, it is important to assess the cost of renovations and upgrades, including materials, labor, and permits. This will help you determine the potential return on your investment, and help you make an informed decision about whether to move forward with the property.

When evaluating potential properties, it is important to consider several key factors. Location, property condition, and potential return on investment are three of the most important considerations.

Location is important because it has a direct impact on the property's value and the ease of selling the property in the future. Properties located in popular, up-and-coming neighborhoods tend to appreciate in value faster than those located in declining areas. Consider the crime rate, proximity to schools and shopping, and access to transportation and other amenities when evaluating a property's location.

The condition of a property is another key factor to consider when evaluating potential investments. Properties in need of significant repairs can be more difficult and expensive to fix, and may not generate the same returns as those in good condition. Consider factors such as the age of the roof, the condition of the plumbing and electrical systems, and the overall state of the interior and exterior of the property when evaluating the condition of a property.

Finally, it is important to consider the potential return on investment when evaluating potential properties. This can be done by calculating the estimated costs of the renovations and the estimated sales price after the renovations are completed. By subtracting the costs from the sales price, you can determine the potential profit. Additionally, consider the time frame for completing the renovations and the costs associated with holding the property during that time.

By considering these key factors and doing proper research, you can identify potential properties that are likely to generate strong returns on investment.

In addition to online resources, it is important to network and build relationships with local real estate professionals such as agents, inspectors, contractors, and lenders. They can provide valuable information and support throughout the house flipping process. In some cases, they may also bring potential properties to your attention before they hit the market.

Another aspect to consider is the location of the property. It is crucial to understand the local market conditions and look for areas with potential for growth and high demand. For example, areas near new developments or amenities, such as parks and shopping centers, are often desirable to buyers.

When evaluating a property, it is important to consider both its potential and its limitations. Start by thoroughly inspecting the property to identify any necessary repairs or renovations. It may also be helpful to get a professional inspection to give a more accurate assessment of the property's condition and potential costs.

Once you have a good understanding of the property, you can use this information to create a budget and timeline for the renovation process. This will help you determine the maximum amount you can afford to spend on the property and ensure that you stay on track throughout the process.

In summary, finding and evaluating properties is a crucial step in the house flipping process and requires careful research, networking, and attention to detail. With the right approach, you can find the right properties to flip and achieve the desired outcomes.

When finding properties to flip, it is important to research the surrounding area and local real estate market. Look for trends in the neighborhood, such as increasing home values or new businesses moving in. This information can help you determine the potential for profit in a given area. It's also important to assess the physical condition of the property, including any necessary repairs or renovations. This can be done through a thorough inspection or by hiring a professional contractor to give you an estimate. Additionally, it's essential to evaluate the property's title and review any outstanding liens or legal issues. Taking these steps can help you determine the potential cost and time investment for a property, and help you make informed decisions about which properties are worth pursuing.

To continue the chapter on "Finding and Evaluating Properties", it's important to consider different methods for locating potential properties for flipping. One of the most popular ways is to use online real estate platforms and websites. These platforms allow you to search for properties based on various criteria such as location, price, and type of property. Another option is to attend local real estate auctions, which are usually held on a regular basis in most cities. At these auctions, you can bid on properties and purchase them for a low price if no one else is bidding.

Additionally, networking with real estate agents and other investors can also be a great way to find potential properties.

Once you've found potential properties, it's important to conduct a thorough evaluation to determine their potential for profit. This evaluation should include a physical inspection of the property, as well as a review of the property's financial and legal status. Some of the things to consider when evaluating a property include:

1. Location: Is the property located in an area that is likely to appreciate in value?

2. Condition: Is the property in good condition, or does it need significant repairs?

3. Market value: What is the current market value of the property and what is the estimated value after repairs?

4. Repair costs: What will it cost to repair and renovate the property?

5. Rental income: Is the property suitable for renting, and what is the estimated monthly rent?

6. Competition: What properties are available in the area, and what are their prices?

7. Financing: What financing options are available, and what will be the cost of borrowing money to purchase the property?

By evaluating each of these factors, you'll be able to determine if the property is worth pursuing as a flipping opportunity. Remember, the goal of flipping a property is to purchase it at a low price, make necessary repairs and renovations, and sell it for a profit. So, it's important to choose properties that have a high potential for profit and a low risk of financial loss.

In this chapter, it is important to discuss the various methods for finding properties to flip. This can include using real estate agents, searching for properties online, attending real estate auctions, or even driving around neighborhoods looking for potential properties.

Once a property is found, it is important to evaluate it properly to determine its potential for flipping. This evaluation process should consider factors such as location, condition of the property, market trends, and potential for renovation or remodeling.

It is also crucial to have a thorough understanding of the local real estate market, including the types of properties that are popular, the average prices for similar properties, and any recent market trends. This information can be obtained through research, speaking with local real estate agents, and reviewing property data available online.

Additionally, it is important to take into account the cost of any necessary renovations or improvements. A detailed renovation budget should be created, which includes materials, labor costs, and any other expenses related to the renovation process.

In conclusion, finding and evaluating properties to flip requires careful consideration and research. With a thorough understanding of the local market and the ability to properly evaluate potential properties, you can increase your chances of success in the house flipping process.

When evaluating potential properties for flipping, it is important to consider factors such as location, property condition, and potential for growth. Researching local real estate trends and neighborhood data can give insight into the property's potential value and future marketability. Conducting a thorough property inspection is also crucial in determining the extent of renovation work needed and the associated costs.

In addition to evaluating the physical aspects of a property, it is important to consider the financial aspects as well. Reviewing property tax records, zoning laws, and permit requirements can help ensure a successful and profitable flip. Understanding the estimated repair costs, holding costs, and potential sale price can give an accurate picture of the potential profits from the flip.

Finally, it is crucial to have a contingency plan in place. Unexpected expenses, zoning changes, and market fluctuations can have an impact on the success of a flip. Having a solid understanding of the local market and potential risks can help minimize these potential issues and ensure a successful and profitable flip.

When evaluating a potential property, it is important to consider its location, age, and overall condition. Location is key when it comes to flipping houses, as it will impact the property's market value and potential resale value. Age is also a factor to consider, as older homes may need more repairs and renovations than newer homes. The overall condition of the property will also play a role in determining the cost and scope of the necessary renovations.

It's also important to consider the local real estate market and the type of property being evaluated. For example, is it a single-family home, a multi-unit building, or a commercial property? Understanding the local real estate market and the type of property being evaluated will help you make informed decisions about what improvements and renovations to make, as well as what the property's value will likely be after those improvements.

Finally, it's important to evaluate the property's financials, including the cost of any necessary repairs and renovations, the potential resale value, and the cost of holding onto the property. This information will help you determine if a potential property is a good investment and if it will generate a profit for you.

In order to make sure you are making a good investment, it's important to properly evaluate a potential property. This includes looking at factors such as its location, the condition of the property, and the cost of necessary repairs.

By considering all of these factors, you'll be able to determine if a property is worth flipping or not.

One important tool you can use in evaluating properties is a property assessment report. This report will give you a detailed overview of the property's condition, including information on its structure, plumbing, electrical systems, and more. You should also take the time to inspect the property yourself, looking for any signs of damage or areas that need improvement.

Another important factor to consider when evaluating properties is the local market. You'll want to research the area, looking at factors such as the average home price, the local economy, and the demand for rental properties. This will help you determine the potential return on investment for a particular property.

By thoroughly evaluating properties, you'll be able to make informed decisions about which properties to flip and which ones to pass on. This will help you maximize your profits and minimize your risk as a real estate investor.

When looking for potential properties to flip, it's important to consider the location of the property. Location can play a major role in determining the value of a property and its potential for appreciation. Look for properties in areas with strong job markets, good schools, and attractive amenities such as parks, shopping centers, and restaurants.

It's also important to consider the condition of the property. Properties in need of extensive repairs can be more challenging and time-consuming to flip, but may offer a greater return on investment if successfully renovated. On the other hand, properties that are in good condition may require fewer repairs, but may have less room for profit.

When evaluating properties, it's crucial to have a detailed understanding of the real estate market in the area, including current trends and economic factors that may impact the market. It's also important to consider the costs associated with flipping a property, including renovations, real estate taxes, and marketing expenses.

Additionally, you may want to consider hiring a real estate agent or appraiser to help with the property evaluation process. They can provide valuable insights into the local real estate market and help you determine the potential value of the property after renovations.

In conclusion, finding and evaluating properties to flip requires a thorough understanding of the real estate market, a keen eye for potential properties, and the ability to accurately assess the costs and potential profits of a potential flip. With these skills and knowledge, you'll be well on your way to success in the world of house flipping.
It's important to perform a thorough evaluation of the property you're considering flipping. This includes inspecting the property inside and out, looking at its foundation, roof, electrical, plumbing and HVAC systems. A comprehensive property evaluation will give you an idea of the cost of repairs and renovations needed to bring the property up to market standards. You can also use this evaluation to determine the property's after-repair value

(ARV), which is the estimated market value of the property after all the repairs and renovations have been made.

You should also consider the property's location and the surrounding neighborhood. Is the property located in a desirable area that is likely to appreciate in value? Are there plans for new development in the area that could potentially increase the property's value? These are important factors to consider when evaluating a property for flipping.

Finally, it's crucial to research any legal or zoning issues that may impact the property. Are there any liens or outstanding debts associated with the property? Are there any zoning restrictions that may impact the property's use or value? These factors can have a significant impact on your flipping project, so it's important to research them thoroughly before making an offer on a property.

When evaluating a property, it is important to consider the location and the surrounding neighborhood. Factors like crime rates, school quality, and local amenities will all impact the future resale value of the property. You should also assess the condition of the property and consider any necessary repairs or renovations that will need to be made.

The condition of the roof, plumbing, electrical, and HVAC systems should all be evaluated, as these can be costly to repair or replace if they are in poor condition. Additionally, it is important to assess the property's foundation, as foundation issues can be extremely expensive to repair and can have a major impact on the overall value of the property.

Another important factor to consider when evaluating a property is the potential for future growth in the surrounding area. Properties in areas with high growth potential are likely to appreciate in value over time, making them a good investment opportunity. You can research potential growth by looking at factors like population growth, job growth, and new developments in the area.

Finally, it is important to consider the cost of the property relative to its estimated resale value. If the cost of the property is significantly less than the estimated resale value, it may be a good investment opportunity. However, if the cost of the property is close to or exceeds the estimated resale value, it may be less of a good investment opportunity.

In conclusion, evaluating properties is a crucial step in the house flipping process and requires a thorough understanding of the property, the surrounding area, and the potential for future growth. With careful consideration and research, you can make informed decisions about which properties to invest in and increase your chances of success in the house flipping market.

Once you have a list of potential properties, it's important to thoroughly evaluate each one to determine its potential as a flip. There are several key factors to consider, including:

Location: Look for properties in desirable areas that are likely to appreciate in value. Consider factors like proximity to schools, parks, public transportation, and shopping centers.

Condition: Assess the condition of the property, including the structure, roof, plumbing, and electrical systems. Consider the cost of repairs needed to bring the property up to standard.

Layout: Consider the layout and flow of the property, including room sizes, number of bedrooms and bathrooms, and whether the property has any unique features that could add value.

Zoning: Check to see if the property is zoned for the intended use and if any zoning changes are in the works that could affect the property's value.

Comparable sales: Research the recent sales prices of similar properties in the area to determine the potential sale price of the property after renovations.

ROI: Calculate the potential return on investment (ROI) by comparing the estimated sale price to the estimated cost of renovations and holding costs.

By taking the time to evaluate properties thoroughly, you can ensure that you are making a wise investment decision. You can also use this information to negotiate a better price and to make informed decisions about the types of renovations that will maximize the property's value.

To sum up, finding and evaluating properties is a critical step in the house flipping process. It requires a thorough understanding of the real estate market, property values, and the condition of the property. It also involves utilizing various tools and techniques such as property search websites, real estate agents, property inspections, and market analysis reports to make informed decisions. In conclusion, having a strong understanding of the market and being able to accurately assess the value and condition of a property is key to finding the right investment property and ensuring a successful flip.

One of the key steps in the house flipping process is finding and evaluating properties that have potential to be purchased, renovated, and sold for a profit. This requires a combination of research, market analysis, and property inspection. Here are some steps to help guide your property search and evaluation.

Determine your target market: Before you start your property search, it's important to have a clear idea of the target market you want to serve. This could be based on factors like location, property type, and the type of renovation work required.

Conduct market research: Research the local real estate market to get a better understanding of current market trends and conditions. This can include looking at data on home sales, price trends, and the current inventory of homes for sale.

The House Flipping Process: A Step-by-Step Guide to Wealth

Use online tools: There are many online tools available that can help you search for properties, including real estate websites, MLS listings, and real estate apps. These tools can help you narrow down your search based on specific criteria such as location, property type, and price range.

Drive the neighborhoods: Spending time driving through target neighborhoods is a great way to get a feel for the area and see what properties are available. You can also get a sense of the local market conditions and the types of homes that are popular.

Network with real estate agents: Building relationships with real estate agents can be a great way to get access to properties that aren't publicly listed. They may be able to provide you with leads on properties that are about to hit the market or that are being sold off-market.

Evaluate properties: Once you've found a property that you're interested in, it's important to evaluate it carefully. This involves conducting a thorough property inspection and assessing the property's potential for renovation and resale. You'll want to consider factors like the property's location, condition, and any potential renovation costs.

Get a property appraisal: Before making an offer on a property, it's important to get a professional appraisal to determine its value. This will help you determine if the property is worth the price you're paying and give you a good starting point for negotiations.

By following these steps, you can increase your chances of finding properties that have the potential to be profitable investments. However, it's important to remember that the process of finding and evaluating properties can be time-consuming, so be prepared to invest the necessary time and effort.

In addition to researching the property and its location, it is also important to understand the financial aspects of flipping a property. Before making an offer on a property, you should have a clear understanding of the estimated costs of any necessary repairs, renovations, or upgrades. This will help you determine whether the property has the potential to generate a profit after all expenses have been taken into account. You should also take into consideration the cost of carrying the property during the renovation process, such as mortgage payments, property taxes, and insurance.

One effective way to evaluate a property's potential is to compare it to similar properties in the area. This can help you understand the market value of the property, as well as the likely resale value of the property after renovations have been completed. You can use online tools, such as Zillow, to view comparable properties and estimate their value. Additionally, it is important to keep up to date with local real estate trends and market conditions. This will give you an understanding of what types of properties are in demand and what features are popular in your target market.

Finally, it is a good idea to work with a real estate professional who can provide valuable insights and information about the property and its location. They can also assist with property inspections, negotiations, and other aspects of the purchasing process. By working with an experienced professional, you can increase your chances of making a profitable investment in house flipping.

In the process of finding and evaluating properties for house flipping, there are several key steps to consider. One of the first steps is to determine the market you want to invest in and to familiarize yourself with the local real estate market. This involves researching various neighborhoods and property types, and understanding the current market conditions, including supply and demand, prices, and trends.

Another important step is to identify potential properties for flipping. This can involve reviewing public records and lists of foreclosures, speaking with real estate agents, and using online tools to find properties that meet your criteria. When evaluating properties, it is essential to look at several factors, including the location, size, condition, and potential for renovation and resale value.

It is also important to consider the cost of the property and the potential return on investment (ROI). To determine the cost of the property, you should factor in the purchase price, the cost of renovations, and any associated fees and expenses, such as closing costs, taxes, and insurance. The ROI can be calculated by subtracting the total cost of the property from the expected resale price and dividing the result by the total cost of the property.

Another important aspect of evaluating properties is to inspect the property thoroughly and assess its condition. This includes checking for any structural or cosmetic damage, verifying the presence of any health or safety hazards, and determining any necessary repairs or renovations. It is also important to assess the overall value of the property and determine if it has the potential to be profitable.

In conclusion, finding and evaluating properties is a critical part of the house flipping process. By thoroughly researching the market, identifying potential properties, and evaluating them carefully, you can increase your chances of success and maximize your returns.

House flipping is a popular real estate investment strategy where investors purchase a property, renovate it, and sell it for a profit. Finding and evaluating properties to flip is a crucial step in the process and requires careful research and analysis. Here are a few key points to keep in mind when finding and evaluating properties:

Location: Location is a key factor to consider when finding properties to flip. Look for areas that are in high demand, have a strong real estate market, and are likely to appreciate in value.

Property type: Consider the type of property you want to flip, such as a single-family home, townhouse, or condo. Each type of property has its own set of pros and cons, so it's important to choose one that fits your investment goals and skillset.

Property condition: Evaluate the condition of the property before making an offer. Consider factors such as the age of the property, the state of the roof, plumbing, electrical systems, and more. Properties in poor condition will require more time, effort, and money to renovate, so be sure to factor that into your budget and timeline.

Comparable sales: Research recent sales of similar properties in the area to get a good understanding of the local real estate market. This information can help you determine a fair price to offer for the property and a realistic timeline for selling it.

Financing options: Consider the financing options available to you, such as a traditional mortgage, a hard money loan, or a private lender. Each option has its own pros and cons, so it's important to choose one that fits your investment goals and financial situation.

By following these steps and conducting thorough research and analysis, you can increase your chances of finding and evaluating properties that are well-suited for flipping and provide a good return on your investment.

When it comes to finding and evaluating properties for flipping, there are several key considerations to keep in mind. Firstly, it is important to research the area where you are looking to invest in, including factors such as the local housing market, employment opportunities, crime rates, and the condition of local schools and amenities. These factors can all impact the desirability of the area and therefore the potential value of any properties you may purchase.

Another important factor to consider when evaluating properties is the condition of the property itself. You should carefully inspect the property inside and out, paying close attention to areas such as the roof, foundations, electrical and plumbing systems, and overall condition of the property. If the property requires significant renovations or repairs, this can greatly impact the time and money required to complete the flip.

It is also crucial to consider the cost of renovations and repairs when evaluating properties. This includes both the cost of materials and labor, as well as any permits or fees that may be required. To help keep costs in check, you may want to consider partnering with a contractor or contractor team who can help provide estimates and keep the project on track.

Finally, when evaluating properties for flipping, it is important to take a long-term view and consider the potential for future appreciation. This means looking at factors such as the growth of the local housing market, trends in property values, and the overall state of the local economy. By taking a long-term view, you can help ensure that your investment in house flipping will pay off in the long run.

In conclusion, when evaluating properties for flipping, it is important to consider a range of factors, including the local area, the condition of the property, the cost of renovations and repairs, and the potential for future appreciation. By carefully considering these factors, you can help ensure that you make informed investment decisions and successfully flip properties for profit.

In order to find and evaluate properties for flipping, it is important to consider the location of the property and the surrounding area. The location of the property should have a high demand for rental or resale properties, as well as good schools, shopping and recreation options. The area should also have a strong job market and low crime rate, which are factors that will attract potential buyers.

Once you have selected a target area, it is important to research the local housing market and keep track of recent sales and rental prices. This will help you get a better understanding of what properties are selling for and what properties are in high demand. Additionally, you should keep an eye out for properties that have been on the market for an extended period of time or have dropped significantly in price, as these properties may be good candidates for flipping.

When evaluating properties, it is important to conduct a thorough inspection to assess the condition of the property and identify any potential issues. This includes evaluating the foundation, roof, plumbing, electrical and heating systems, as well as the overall condition of the interior and exterior of the property. You should also consider the cost of any necessary repairs or renovations, and factor this into your purchase price.

Another important factor to consider when evaluating properties is the zoning and building codes in the area. Properties located in areas with strict zoning laws may be more difficult to flip, as you may be required to make expensive renovations in order to comply with local building codes. On the other hand, properties located in areas with more relaxed building codes may be easier to flip, as you may be able to make renovations with less red tape.

In conclusion, finding and evaluating properties for flipping requires research, due diligence and careful consideration of a number of factors. By taking the time to research the local housing market, inspect properties thoroughly and consider the zoning and building codes in the area, you can help ensure that you select the right properties for flipping and achieve your investment goals.

When it comes to finding and evaluating properties for house flipping, there are several important steps to follow. First, you will want to determine the types of properties that are most likely to be profitable in your area. This will often involve researching local real estate trends, including the demand for different types of properties and the average sales prices for those properties.

Next, you will need to identify potential properties that you would like to evaluate. This can be done through a variety of methods, including driving through neighborhoods and searching online real estate listings. You should also consider reaching out to real estate agents and other professionals in your area who may be able to provide you with additional information about properties that may be of interest to you.

Once you have identified a property that you would like to evaluate, you will need to perform a thorough analysis to determine whether it is a good investment opportunity. This will typically involve evaluating the property's current condition, its location and neighborhood, and the surrounding market conditions. You may also want to consider hiring a professional inspector to perform a more detailed evaluation of the property, including a thorough inspection of the property's structure and systems.

It is also important to consider the costs of any repairs or renovations that may be necessary in order to bring the property up to a condition that will attract potential buyers. You should create a detailed budget that takes into account the cost of all necessary repairs, as well as any other costs associated with the property, such as closing costs, property taxes, and insurance.

Finally, once you have fully evaluated the property and determined that it is a good investment opportunity, you will need to negotiate the purchase price and finalize the transaction. This may involve working with a real estate agent or attorney, as well as obtaining any necessary financing.

By following these steps, you can effectively find and evaluate properties for house flipping and increase your chances of success in this exciting and lucrative industry.

The House Flipping Process: A Step-by-Step Guide to Wealth

House flipping is a popular investment strategy where individuals purchase an undervalued property, make repairs and renovations, and then sell it for a profit. Finding and evaluating properties is a crucial step in this process. The following are some of the key factors to consider when searching for and evaluating properties for flipping:

Location: The location of a property can significantly impact its value and desirability. Factors such as proximity to schools, shopping, transportation, and other amenities, as well as the overall safety and appeal of the neighborhood, should be taken into account when choosing a property to flip.

Property condition: A property's condition will play a big role in determining the level of work and cost required to make it market-ready. Properties that are in need of extensive repairs and renovations will require more time and resources, but also offer more potential for profit if done correctly.

Market trends: It's important to stay up-to-date on market trends and conditions. Understanding local real estate trends and the current demand for specific types of properties, such as single-family homes or multi-unit properties, can help guide your search for the right property to flip.

Demographic data: Demographic information about the local area can also be useful in determining the demand for a particular property type. Understanding the average income levels, age group, and family size in the area can help you make informed decisions about which properties are most likely to sell quickly and for a good profit.

Price and competition: Finally, evaluating the price and competition in the market is crucial when searching for a property to flip. Knowing what similar properties have sold for in the area and the level of competition for flipping properties in the market can help you determine the maximum price you should be willing to pay for a property.

By taking the time to evaluate these factors, you can ensure that you are making an informed decision when choosing a property to flip.

Finding and evaluating properties is one of the most critical aspects of house flipping. It involves a thorough analysis of the market and the properties themselves to determine the best investment opportunities. To find properties, investors can start by searching online through real estate listings, attending real estate auctions, or working with real estate agents. They can also attend local events and open houses to meet potential sellers and get a firsthand look at the properties.

Once the potential properties are identified, it's essential to evaluate them carefully. The first step is to assess the location. Location is key when it comes to house flipping, and it's important to consider factors such as crime rate, the quality of schools, and proximity to amenities. The condition of the property should also be evaluated. This includes a review of the physical structure, as well as any repairs or renovations that may be needed.

Another important consideration is the price of the property. Investors should be aware of the current market values of similar properties in the area, and take into account any improvements or upgrades that could increase the value of the property. In addition to the purchase price, it's also essential to consider the cost of any repairs or renovations, as well as the expected holding costs, such as property taxes and utilities.

Finally, investors should consider the potential return on investment. This includes the expected profit margins, as well as the time it will take to sell the property. The faster the property can be sold, the lower the holding costs and the better the return on investment. With careful evaluation and analysis, investors can find the best properties to flip and maximize their profits.

Finding and evaluating properties for flipping purposes can be a complex and time-consuming process, but it is critical to the success of any house flipping project. The first step in finding properties is to determine the target market. This includes considering factors such as location, property type, and target demographic. Once a target market has been established, it is important to research and analyze real estate data to identify potential properties. This data can be obtained from various sources, including online real estate databases, local real estate agents, and government agencies.

Once potential properties have been identified, it is important to conduct a thorough evaluation of each property to determine its potential for profit. This evaluation should include a careful examination of the property's condition, including its structure, electrical and plumbing systems, and overall condition. It is also important to consider any necessary repairs or renovations that may be required, as well as the estimated costs of these repairs.

In addition to the physical condition of the property, it is also important to consider other factors that may impact its potential for profit, such as zoning restrictions, neighborhood trends, and local market conditions. This information can be obtained through research, including online resources and consultation with real estate experts and professionals.

When evaluating potential properties, it is important to have a clear understanding of the overall flipping market, including current trends and conditions. This information can be obtained through research, including online real estate data, local real estate market reports, and consultation with professionals in the industry.

Ultimately, the success of any house flipping project depends on finding and evaluating the right properties. This requires a combination of research, analysis, and intuition, as well as a willingness to take calculated risks. With careful evaluation and analysis, however, it is possible to identify and successfully flip properties that can provide significant returns on investment.

The House Flipping Process: A Step-by-Step Guide to Wealth

In the process of finding and evaluating properties, it is essential to have a clear understanding of your goals and investment strategy. This will help you determine the type of properties you are interested in and the areas you want to focus on.

One way to start is by researching the local real estate market, including the prices of comparable properties, recent sales trends, and the demand for rental properties in the area. This information can be obtained through online resources, real estate agents, and property management companies.

Once you have identified potential properties, it is important to perform a thorough property evaluation. This includes inspecting the property for any physical and structural issues, as well as evaluating the property's financials, such as rental income and expenses. A professional inspection can provide valuable insights into the property's condition and potential for renovation.

In addition to the physical inspection, it is also important to review the property's legal and financial documents, including title reports, deeds, and zoning regulations. This will help ensure that there are no legal or financial issues with the property that could impact your investment.

Finally, it is important to have a clear understanding of the property's potential for appreciation and rental income. This will help you determine the property's potential return on investment and whether it is a good fit for your investment strategy.

Overall, finding and evaluating properties is a critical step in the house flipping process. By performing a thorough analysis and due diligence, you can help ensure that you make informed and profitable investment decisions.

When flipping houses, it is crucial to have a clear understanding of the property you are interested in buying. There are several steps involved in finding and evaluating properties, including:

Defining your target market: Start by identifying the type of properties you are interested in and the areas where you want to invest. You can look for properties in areas with high demand, strong rental demand, or a high rate of appreciation.

Searching for properties: Use online real estate platforms, classified websites, or work with a real estate agent to find potential properties. You can also drive through neighborhoods and look for distressed properties that might be suitable for flipping.

Conducting property inspections: Once you have found a potential property, arrange to have it inspected by a professional inspector. This will help you determine any necessary repairs or renovations, and provide you with an estimated cost for those improvements.

Evaluating the property's financials: Look at the property's financial history, including its previous sales, property taxes, and any liens or judgments against the property. You will also want to consider the estimated costs for repairs, renovations, and holding costs.

Completing a market analysis: Use local real estate data and market trends to estimate the potential resale value of the property. Take into account the location, competition, and other relevant factors when determining your estimated resale price.

By following these steps, you can ensure that you are making a well-informed decision when investing in a property to flip. Remember, the success of a flip is largely dependent on finding the right property, so take your time to evaluate all your options before making a final decision.

In conclusion, finding and evaluating properties is a crucial step in the house flipping process. It requires research, analysis, and a thorough understanding of the local real estate market. By using various tools and techniques, investors can determine which properties have the greatest potential for profitability and minimize the risk of financial losses. However, it is important to keep in mind that every real estate market is unique, and what works in one area may not work in another. As a result, it is always important to stay up-to-date with the latest market trends and conditions in order to make informed decisions. With careful planning and due diligence, investors can successfully find and evaluate properties that will provide high returns on their investments.

"Opportunities are everywhere, but it's up to us to find and evaluate the right ones."

The House Flipping Process: A Step-by-Step Guide to Wealth

Chapter 4

Renovation Planning and Management

Renovation planning and management is a crucial step in the house flipping process. It requires careful planning and execution to ensure that the renovation project stays on track, within budget and ultimately results in a profitable flip. In this chapter, we will discuss the key steps in renovation planning and management.

Establishing a budget and timeline: The first step in renovation planning is to establish a budget and timeline for the project. This will help you determine how much money you need to allocate for materials, labor, and any unexpected expenses. It is also important to establish a realistic timeline for the project so that you can ensure that it is completed within a reasonable time frame.

Assessing the property: Before you begin the renovation process, it is important to thoroughly assess the property to determine the extent of the work that needs to be done. This will help you identify any potential problems and make sure that you have a clear plan for the renovation process.

Hiring contractors: Hiring the right contractors is a crucial step in the renovation process. You should only work with contractors who have experience in the type of work that you need done, and who have a good reputation in the industry. You should also get written quotes from each contractor to ensure that you have a clear understanding of the costs involved.

Managing the renovation project: Once the renovation project is underway, it is important to manage it closely to ensure that it stays on track. This includes regularly reviewing the budget, checking in on the contractors, and addressing any problems that arise in a timely manner.

Inspection and final touches: Once the renovation is complete, it is important to conduct a thorough inspection of the property to ensure that all of the work has been completed to a high standard. Any final touches, such as painting, cleaning, and landscaping, should also be completed before the property is put on the market.

In conclusion, proper planning and management is crucial to the success of a house flipping project. By following these steps, you can ensure that your renovation project is completed on time, within budget, and results in a profitable flip.

In addition to finding and evaluating properties, a crucial part of the house flipping process is renovation planning and management. The renovation plan should take into account the scope of work, budget, timeline, and materials needed to complete the project. It is essential to have a clear understanding of the cost and timeline of each project, as this will help ensure that the project stays on budget and on schedule.

One important aspect of renovation planning is to prioritize the necessary repairs and renovations. For example, structural issues such as a damaged foundation or a leaky roof should be addressed first, as they can negatively impact the value of the property and make it difficult to sell. Other cosmetic renovations, such as updating a bathroom or kitchen, can be done after the more critical repairs are completed.

A project manager or contractor should be hired to oversee the renovation work, as they have the experience and expertise to ensure the work is completed correctly and efficiently. The project manager or contractor should be responsible for supervising the construction crew, ordering materials, and ensuring that the work is completed according to the renovation plan.

Another important aspect of renovation management is effective communication with all stakeholders involved, including the project manager, contractor, and any sub-contractors. It is essential to establish clear lines of communication and to ensure that everyone is on the same page regarding the scope of work, timeline, and budget.

In conclusion, proper planning and management of renovations are essential to the success of a house flipping project. By taking the time to develop a comprehensive renovation plan, prioritize necessary repairs and renovations, and establish clear lines of communication, house flippers can increase their chances of success and minimize the risk of delays or cost overruns.

When planning a renovation project, it is crucial to have a clear budget in mind. A budget helps you stay on track and prevents unexpected costs from popping up. When determining your budget, be sure to consider all aspects of the renovation, including materials, labor, permits, and any upgrades you may want to make.

Once you have your budget in place, it is important to create a timeline for the renovation. This timeline should include the start and end dates for each stage of the renovation, as well as the estimated time for each task. Having a timeline helps keep the project on track and ensures that deadlines are met.

The next step in renovation planning and management is to choose a contractor. It is important to find a contractor who has experience with similar renovation projects and who is able to complete the work within your budget and timeline. When selecting a contractor, be sure to get several quotes and compare them before making a decision.

Once the contractor has been selected, it is important to have a clear understanding of their responsibilities. This can include tasks such as obtaining necessary permits, ordering materials, and supervising the workers. Make sure to have a written contract in place that outlines the responsibilities of each party.

During the renovation, it is important to have regular check-ins with the contractor to ensure that the project is progressing as planned. This is also a good time to address any issues or concerns that may have arisen.

Finally, after the renovation is complete, it is important to conduct a final walk-through to ensure that all work has been completed to your satisfaction. If there are any issues or discrepancies, it is best to address them now before final payment is made.

In conclusion, renovation planning and management requires careful planning, budgeting, and communication. By following these steps, you can ensure that your renovation project is completed on time and within budget.

Renovating a property can be a complex and time-consuming process, but with proper planning and management, it can also be a rewarding and profitable endeavor. Before embarking on a renovation project, it is important to have a clear understanding of the scope of work, budget, timeline, and potential risks and challenges.

The first step in renovation planning is to determine the goals and objectives of the project. This includes considering factors such as the desired end result, budget constraints, and any necessary changes to the property's layout or design. Once these objectives are established, it is important to develop a detailed renovation plan, which includes a budget, timeline, and scope of work.

Next, it is essential to assemble a team of professionals, including a general contractor, architect, and tradespeople. This team will be responsible for overseeing the renovation process and ensuring that all work is completed according to the plan. It is important to thoroughly vet potential contractors and tradespeople to ensure that they have the experience and expertise necessary to complete the job.

Once the renovation plan is in place, it is crucial to implement a system for monitoring and managing the project. This includes tracking the progress of the work, managing the budget, and communicating with the team and stakeholders. A project management system, such as a software program or spreadsheet, can be helpful in keeping the project on track and ensuring that all deadlines are met.

Another important aspect of renovation planning is risk management. This involves identifying potential risks, such as budget overruns, construction delays, or unforeseen issues, and developing contingency plans to minimize the impact of these risks. For example, a contingency plan might include a reserve fund to cover unexpected expenses, or a backup timeline in case of construction delays.

Finally, it is important to consider the legal and regulatory requirements of the renovation project. This includes obtaining the necessary permits and approvals, ensuring that all work is completed in accordance with building codes and regulations, and addressing any environmental or health and safety concerns.

In conclusion, proper renovation planning and management is essential for ensuring that a renovation project is completed on time, within budget, and to the desired standards. By taking the time to plan and manage the project carefully, investors and property owners can reap the benefits of a successful renovation and increase the value of their property.

Renovation planning and management is a critical aspect of real estate investment. It involves creating a plan for improving or upgrading an existing property to increase its value and make it more attractive to potential tenants or buyers. A well-planned renovation project can significantly improve the profitability of an investment property, but it's important to approach it carefully and methodically to ensure success.

One important step in renovation planning is to conduct a thorough assessment of the property to identify its strengths and weaknesses. This assessment should consider the physical condition of the property, the layout and design of the living spaces, the age of major systems and appliances, and the overall aesthetic appeal of the property. Based on this information, you can create a prioritized list of renovations that need to be made to the property in order to achieve your goals.

Next, you should create a detailed budget for the renovation project, including all expected costs, such as labor, materials, permits, and fees. This budget should also include a contingency plan for unexpected expenses that may arise during the renovation process. It's important to have a realistic budget in place before starting the renovation process so that you can stay on track and avoid costly overages or delays.

Once you have a clear plan and budget in place, the next step is to select a contractor to carry out the renovations. It's important to choose a contractor with experience in property renovations who is licensed and insured. You should also check references, ask for proof of insurance, and review their portfolio of completed projects before hiring a contractor.

During the renovation process, it's important to stay actively involved in the project to ensure that it is being completed on time, within budget, and to your satisfaction. This may involve regular check-ins with the contractor, making decisions on materials and finishes, and making adjustments to the plan as necessary.

To illustrate, consider the renovation of a rental property that has outdated kitchens and bathrooms. The property assessment reveals that these two areas are the most important to focus on to improve the overall appeal and value of the property. A budget is created that includes the cost of new appliances, fixtures, flooring, and cabinetry. A reputable contractor is hired, and during the renovation process, the property owner makes decisions on the type of appliances and finishes to be used, and the contractor provides regular updates on the progress of the work.

By following a thorough process for renovation planning and management, real estate investors can ensure that their renovation projects are completed efficiently, within budget, and to their satisfaction. With careful planning and attention to detail, a well-executed renovation project can have a significant impact on the value and profitability of an investment property.

Renovating a property can be a complex process that requires careful planning and management. To ensure a successful renovation project, it is important to start by setting clear goals and a budget. This will help to guide the project and keep it on track.

One key aspect of renovation planning is to assess the existing condition of the property. This will help to identify any structural or cosmetic issues that need to be addressed, and to determine what renovations will be necessary to achieve the desired goals. For example, if the goal is to increase energy efficiency, a property assessment might identify issues such as poor insulation, leaky windows, or outdated heating and cooling systems that need to be addressed.

Once the property assessment has been completed, it is important to create a detailed renovation plan that outlines the scope of work, a timeline for completion, and a budget. This plan should include a detailed breakdown of all of the costs associated with the renovation, including materials, labor, and any permits that may be required.

When it comes to managing a renovation project, it is essential to work with experienced professionals who have the skills and knowledge necessary to ensure a successful outcome. For example, it is important to choose a reputable contractor who has experience working on similar projects and who can provide references and examples of their work. Additionally, it may be necessary to work with other professionals, such as architects, engineers, and designers, to ensure that the renovation is done correctly and meets all necessary building codes and regulations.

Finally, it is important to communicate regularly with all of the professionals involved in the renovation project to ensure that everyone is on the same page and that the project stays on track. This can be done through regular meetings, phone calls, or email updates, and should involve a clear discussion of any issues or challenges that arise during the renovation process.

In conclusion, renovating a property can be a complex and challenging process, but with careful planning and management, it can also be a rewarding and successful endeavor. By setting clear goals and a budget, assessing the existing condition of the property, creating a detailed renovation plan, working with experienced professionals, and communicating regularly throughout the project, it is possible to ensure a successful renovation outcome.

Renovating a property can be a complex and time-consuming process, but with proper planning and management, it can also be a rewarding and profitable experience. Here are a few key steps and considerations to keep in mind when planning and managing a renovation project:

Set a budget: Determine how much you are willing to spend on the renovation, taking into account all of the costs involved, including materials, labor, and contingency funds for unexpected expenses.

Hire a contractor: Consider hiring a contractor who is experienced in managing renovation projects, has a good reputation, and is licensed and insured. It is important to get references and check their portfolio before hiring.

Determine the scope of work: Decide what renovations you want to do and what your goals are for the project. Consider the impact of each renovation on the rest of the property and prioritize them based on importance and feasibility.

Create a timeline: Work with your contractor to create a timeline for the renovation project, including milestones and deadlines. This will help keep the project on track and ensure that it is completed on time and within budget.

Manage the project: Regularly check in with the contractor and ensure that the work is being completed to your satisfaction. If any changes or issues arise, work with the contractor to resolve them quickly and efficiently.

Inspect and test: Before completing the project, inspect all the work and test all systems to ensure that they are working properly. Make any final adjustments as needed, and take the time to thoroughly clean and tidy up the property.

Celebrate completion: After the project is complete, take time to celebrate the successful completion of your renovation project and enjoy the fruits of your labor.

Examples of renovation projects include kitchen and bathroom upgrades, adding a room or deck, repainting, installing new flooring, and updating electrical or plumbing systems. The key to success with renovation projects is to plan carefully, communicate effectively with your contractor, and remain flexible throughout the process to accommodate changes and unexpected challenges.

Renovating a property can be a complex process that involves multiple stages and various tasks to be completed. Effective planning and management of the renovation project can help ensure that it is completed on time, within budget, and to the desired quality standards.

One key aspect of renovation planning and management is determining the scope of the project. This involves clearly defining what work needs to be done, and determining the time, cost, and resources required to complete it. This information can be used to develop a detailed project plan and budget, which can help ensure that the renovation project stays on track.

Another important aspect of renovation planning and management is selecting the right contractors and suppliers. It is important to choose contractors who are experienced, skilled, and have a proven track record of delivering quality work. Before hiring contractors, it is a good idea to obtain quotes from several different contractors, compare their prices and services, and choose the one that best meets your needs and budget.

Project management is also critical to the success of a renovation project. A project manager can help ensure that the project stays on schedule and within budget, and can help coordinate the work of different contractors and suppliers. In addition, regular communication with the contractors, suppliers, and property owners can help keep everyone informed of progress and resolve any issues that arise during the renovation process.

Finally, it is important to have a contingency plan in place in case of unexpected problems or delays. This could include having extra funding available to cover unexpected expenses, or having backup plans in place in case a particular contractor or supplier is unable to complete their work.

Examples of successful renovation planning and management include the renovation of a historic building, the conversion of an office building into residential units, and the upgrade of an existing property to make it more energy-efficient and environmentally friendly. In each of these cases, effective planning, project management, and communication helped ensure that the renovation project was completed on time, within budget, and to the desired quality standards.

Renovation projects can range from small cosmetic upgrades to major overhauls of a property. Regardless of the scale of the project, careful planning and management is crucial for success. Here are a few key factors to consider in the planning and management process:

Determine the scope of the project: Before starting any renovation work, it's important to have a clear understanding of the scope of the project. This includes what areas of the property need to be renovated, the type of work required, and the timeline for completion.

Set a budget: Renovations can be expensive, so it's important to have a clear budget in mind. This should include not only the cost of materials and labor, but also any additional expenses such as permits, inspections, and contingency funds.

Hire a team: Depending on the scope of the project, you may need to hire a team of professionals to assist with the renovation work. This could include contractors, architects, designers, and engineers. It's important to choose experienced professionals who have a good reputation and can provide references.

Obtain necessary permits: Depending on the type of work being done, you may need to obtain various permits from local government agencies. For example, if you're making structural changes to the property, you may need a building permit.

Create a timeline: Once the scope of the project and budget are determined, it's important to create a detailed timeline for the work. This should include milestones, deadlines, and any key dates such as inspections or permit approvals.

Monitor progress: Regularly monitoring progress on the renovation project is crucial for ensuring that the work is being done on time and within budget. This may involve regular meetings with the renovation team, as well as inspections of the work as it progresses.

By following these steps and being proactive in the planning and management of a renovation project, you can help ensure its success.

Renovating a property can be a complex and time-consuming process, but with proper planning and management, it can also be a rewarding one. To start, a property owner should develop a clear understanding of their renovation goals, budget, and timeline. This will help guide the decision-making process and ensure that the project stays on track.

Once a plan is in place, it is important to carefully select a team of professionals to help with the renovation. This can include contractors, architects, engineers, and interior designers, depending on the scope of the project. It is essential to thoroughly research and vet these professionals, checking references and ensuring they have the necessary licenses and insurance.

During the renovation process, regular progress updates and communication with the team is crucial. This can help to identify and address any issues that arise in a timely manner, and keep the project moving forward smoothly. It is also important to have contingency plans in place in case of any unexpected problems, such as delays or budget overruns.

Finally, proper documentation is key to successful renovation planning and management. This includes keeping detailed records of all expenses, contracts, and communication with the team, as well as creating a comprehensive project timeline and checklist. These records can help to ensure that the renovation runs smoothly and can also serve as valuable reference materials in the future.

For example, a homeowner wants to renovate their kitchen. They set a budget of $30,000 and a timeline of 4 months. They research and select a team of contractors, architects, and interior designers. The homeowner regularly communicates with the team and stays informed about progress updates. They also keep detailed records of expenses, contracts, and communication. The kitchen renovation is completed within budget and on time, and the homeowner is pleased with the end result.

Another aspect of renovation planning and management is budgeting. It's important to have a clear understanding of how much money you have to work with, and how much each aspect of the renovation will cost. This can be done by obtaining quotes from contractors and suppliers, and by researching costs for materials and labor. Once you have a good understanding of the costs involved, you can start to prioritize what is most important to you and what can be cut if necessary. For example, you may decide to spend more on a high-end kitchen renovation, but compromise on the bathroom tiles.

Project management is another key aspect of renovation planning and management. A good project manager will help keep the renovation on track, and ensure that the various tradespeople and contractors are working together effectively. They will also help to resolve any issues that arise, and keep the renovation on budget. This person could be a general contractor, an architect, or a dedicated project manager.

Finally, it's important to have a clear timeline for the renovation. This will help to keep everyone on track and ensure that the project is completed within a reasonable timeframe. The timeline should include not just the work that needs to be done, but also the order in which it should be done. For example, it may not make sense to install new windows before the walls have been repainted, or to install new flooring before the walls have been re-plastered. A clear timeline will help to ensure that the renovation runs smoothly and that there are no delays.

In conclusion, renovation planning and management is a complex process that requires careful consideration and attention to detail. By taking the time to plan, budget, and manage the renovation, you can ensure that the end result is exactly what you want, and that the renovation is completed within a reasonable timeframe and budget.

When it comes to renovation planning and management, it's important to consider all the factors that may impact the renovation project. For example, budget constraints, building codes, and available resources should all be considered when planning and managing a renovation project. Additionally, it is important to choose the right contractors, as well as to manage the time frame of the renovation project so that it can be completed within budget and on time.

One of the most important factors in renovation planning is budget. It is essential to determine the total budget for the renovation project before the project begins. This will help to ensure that the project remains within budget and that there are no surprises at the end of the project. For example, if the total budget for a renovation project is $50,000, it is important to make sure that this amount is enough to cover all of the necessary expenses, such as materials, labor, and any other costs that may arise during the project.

Building codes are another important factor to consider when planning and managing a renovation project. It is important to be aware of the local building codes in your area, as well as to make sure that the renovation project complies with these codes. For example, if a building is being renovated to include an addition, it is important to make sure that the addition complies with local building codes, such as those related to the height of the addition and the type of materials used.

The selection of contractors is also an important factor in renovation planning and management. When choosing contractors, it is important to choose those who have experience in the type of renovation project you are undertaking, as well as to choose contractors who are licensed and insured. Additionally, it is important to get references from previous clients and to check the contractors' references to ensure that they have a good reputation and that they have completed similar projects to the one you are undertaking.

Finally, it is important to manage the time frame of the renovation project. This can be done by setting realistic deadlines for each stage of the project, as well as by monitoring the progress of the project to ensure that it remains on track. For example, if a renovation project is expected to take six months to complete, it is important to set deadlines for each stage of the project, such as the completion of the demolition stage, the completion of the framing stage, and so on. Additionally, it is important to monitor the progress of the project to ensure that it remains on track and that it is completed on time.

Project management software such as Asana, Trello, and Microsoft Project can also be used to plan and track the progress of a renovation project. These tools provide a visual representation of the project timeline, as well as a platform to communicate with the contractor and other stakeholders. For example, a homeowner can create a renovation project in Asana, assign tasks to the contractor, set deadlines, and track the progress of each task. This allows the homeowner to stay informed about the project and ensure that everything is progressing according to plan.

In addition to project management software, it is also important to have clear communication with the contractor. This includes setting expectations for project timelines, outlining the scope of the project, and addressing any issues that arise during the renovation. The homeowner should also review the contract carefully and be aware of their rights and responsibilities in the event of any disputes.

Finally, it is crucial to have a contingency plan in place in case of unexpected events or emergencies. This may include having extra funds set aside for unexpected expenses, having a backup plan in case of weather-related delays, or having a plan in place to address any structural issues that may arise during the renovation.

In conclusion, renovation planning and management involves careful consideration of the scope of the project, budget, timeline, and resources. By using project management software, having clear communication with the contractor, and having a contingency plan in place, homeowners can ensure that their renovation project is a success and results in the desired outcome.

It is important to have a clear budget and timeline for your renovation project. This will help you stay on track and avoid unexpected expenses. For example, if you plan to renovate your bathroom, you should consider the cost of materials such as tiles, fixtures, and cabinets. You should also factor in the cost of labor, such as the cost of hiring a contractor or plumber. It is a good idea to get several quotes from different contractors to ensure that you are getting a fair price for the work.

Another important aspect of renovation planning and management is communication with your contractors. This can involve setting up regular progress meetings to ensure that the work is progressing according to schedule, as well as addressing any issues that may arise during the renovation process. For example, if there are any unexpected problems with the plumbing or electrical systems, it is important to discuss these with your contractor and find a solution as soon as possible.

It is also important to consider the impact that your renovation will have on the surrounding area. For example, if you are renovating a kitchen, you will need to consider the impact that this will have on the rest of your home, such as increased noise levels or disruptions to your daily routine. To mitigate these effects, you may need to temporarily relocate to another room or arrange for alternative cooking arrangements.

Finally, it is important to have a contingency plan in place in case the renovation project encounters any setbacks or delays. This may involve having backup contractors on standby or having a plan in place to temporarily relocate if necessary. With proper planning and management, however, the renovation process can be a smooth and enjoyable experience.

Another key aspect of renovation planning and management is budgeting. Establishing a budget and sticking to it is crucial in order to ensure the success of the renovation project. A budget will help to determine the scope of the renovation project and what can realistically be accomplished within the given budget.

It is important to prioritize the most important elements of the renovation first and allocate the budget accordingly. For example, if the kitchen is in dire need of an upgrade, then a larger portion of the budget should be allocated towards the kitchen renovation.

It is also essential to allocate a contingency budget for unforeseen expenses that may arise during the renovation process. These can include unexpected repairs, changes in the scope of the project, or even price increases for materials and labor. A contingency budget of 10-20% of the overall budget is recommended to ensure that the project can be completed successfully.

Example: If the total budget for a renovation project is $100,000, a contingency budget of $10,000 to $20,000 can be allocated for unexpected expenses.

Finally, it is important to review and compare quotes from multiple contractors to ensure that the best possible deal is being obtained for the renovation project. It is also important to thoroughly vet each contractor and read reviews to ensure that they are reputable and have a history of successful renovation projects.

In conclusion, renovation planning and management is a complex process that requires careful planning and attention to detail. By setting a budget, prioritizing the most important elements of the renovation, and thoroughly researching contractors, a successful renovation project can be achieved.

When planning and managing a renovation project, it is important to consider various factors and make informed decisions throughout the process. For example, it is important to consider the timeline of the project, the budget, and the required permits and approvals. Here are a few tips to help with the planning and management of a renovation project:

Set a realistic timeline: Before starting the project, it is important to set a realistic timeline for completion. This will help to ensure that the project is completed on time and within budget. Be sure to factor in time for unforeseen events, such as inclement weather or unexpected delays.

Hire the right professionals: Hiring the right professionals can greatly impact the success of a renovation project. Look for contractors who have experience in the specific type of renovation you are planning and who have a good reputation in the industry.

Establish a clear budget: Establishing a clear budget for the renovation project is crucial for ensuring that costs do not spiral out of control. Be sure to include a contingency fund for unexpected expenses. Consider using a cost estimating software to help you determine the cost of the project.

Obtain necessary permits and approvals: Depending on the type of renovation, you may need to obtain permits and approvals from local authorities. Ensure that all necessary permits are in place before starting the project to avoid any legal or financial issues.

Regular progress updates: Regular progress updates are important to keep track of the progress of the project and ensure that it is on track. Hold regular meetings with contractors and suppliers to discuss any challenges and resolve any issues.

Quality control: It is important to have a quality control plan in place to ensure that the work is completed to a high standard. Consider conducting regular inspections to check that the work is up to the expected standard.

By considering these factors and making informed decisions throughout the process, you can ensure that your renovation project runs smoothly and is completed to your satisfaction.

The renovation planning and management process is a crucial aspect of property investment. By following a structured approach, investors can ensure that their renovation projects are completed on time, within budget, and to a high standard of quality.

This includes conducting a thorough assessment of the property, creating a detailed renovation plan, selecting a competent team of professionals, and effectively managing the project from start to finish.

With careful planning and effective management, investors can maximize their return on investment and add value to their properties, leading to long-term financial success.

"The art of renovation is to balance design, function, and budget to create a home that is not only beautiful, but also livable and affordable."

Chapter 5

Marketing and Selling Properties

Marketing and selling properties require a well-coordinated effort to reach potential buyers and effectively communicate the value and unique selling points of a property. The following is a comprehensive guide on marketing and selling properties:

Determine the target market: Identifying the target market is the first and most important step in the marketing process. Factors such as location, age, income, family size, and lifestyle should be considered to determine the target market.

Develop a marketing plan: A marketing plan is a written document that outlines the steps necessary to promote the property and reach the target market. The plan should include a budget, the media channels to be used, and the specific tactics that will be employed to reach the target market.

The House Flipping Process: A Step-by-Step Guide to Wealth

Prepare the property: Before marketing the property, it is important to prepare it for sale. This includes cleaning, decluttering, and making any necessary repairs. If the property is in poor condition, it may be necessary to invest in a professional staging company to help present it in the best light possible.

Use professional photography and videography: High-quality photography and videography are essential for effective property marketing. These visual materials should showcase the property's best features and highlight its unique selling points.

Utilize online and offline marketing channels: Online marketing channels include websites, social media, and online classifieds. Offline marketing channels include print advertising, direct mail, and signage. Both online and offline channels should be used to reach the target market and generate interest in the property.

Open houses and showings: Open houses and showings provide an opportunity for potential buyers to see the property in person and get a feel for its features and layout. These events should be well-coordinated and well-attended, with refreshments and informational materials available for prospective buyers.

Price the property appropriately: Pricing a property appropriately is critical to attracting the right buyers and ensuring a successful sale. A real estate professional can help determine the correct asking price based on market conditions and the property's unique features.

Negotiate the sale: When a buyer makes an offer, the next step is to negotiate the sale. This may involve some back-and-forth between the buyer and seller, and a real estate professional can help facilitate this process to ensure a successful sale.

Marketing and selling properties is a complex process that requires a deep understanding of the target market, effective marketing strategies, and the ability to negotiate a successful sale. With careful planning and a commitment to excellence, properties can be marketed and sold effectively to reach the right buyers and generate positive results.

Marketing and selling properties is a critical part of the real estate business. The objective is to reach potential buyers and sell the property at the best price possible. Marketing can be done in various ways, including online advertising, traditional advertising, open houses, and more. The following are a few examples of successful marketing strategies for properties:

Online Advertising: The use of online platforms like websites, social media, and real estate apps has become increasingly popular for property marketing. This allows for a wider reach, as people from different locations can access the information online. For example, a property owner can create a website specifically for their property, with detailed information about the property, including photos, videos, floor plans, and more.

Traditional Advertising: This includes methods such as newspaper and magazine advertisements, billboards, and radio commercials. Although this is not as popular as online advertising, it can still be an effective way to reach potential buyers. For example, a property owner could place an advertisement in a local newspaper or real estate magazine to reach potential buyers in the area.

Open Houses: Open houses are an effective way to market a property and attract potential buyers. During an open house, potential buyers can see the property in person, ask questions, and get a feel for the property. This can help to generate interest and create a positive impression of the property. For example, a property owner could host an open house and provide refreshments for attendees to create a welcoming atmosphere.

Referral Marketing: This involves leveraging relationships and word of mouth to generate interest in a property. For example, a property owner could ask their friends, family members, and colleagues to share information about the property with others who may be interested in buying. This can be an effective way to reach potential buyers and generate interest in a property.

In conclusion, successful marketing and selling of properties requires a comprehensive approach that includes various strategies. It is important to reach potential buyers and generate interest in a property to achieve the best possible results.

Marketing and Selling Properties is a critical step in real estate investing. It is the process of attracting potential buyers and presenting a property in the best possible light to close a sale. Here are a few key points to consider when marketing and selling properties:

Determine the target market: Identifying the target market for a property is crucial. This includes understanding the demographics, lifestyle, and purchasing habits of potential buyers. This information can be gathered through market research, property assessments, and feedback from real estate agents.

Price the property correctly: Pricing a property correctly is essential to attracting potential buyers and closing a sale. Factors such as location, condition, and market demand can impact the price. It is important to work with a real estate agent to determine a fair market value for the property.

Create appealing marketing materials: Marketing materials such as flyers, brochures, and virtual tours can help attract potential buyers. These materials should highlight the property's unique features and benefits, and showcase its best qualities. High-quality photography and well-written descriptions can also play a key role in attracting potential buyers.

Utilize online marketing platforms: The internet has revolutionized the real estate market. Utilizing online marketing platforms such as real estate websites, social media, and online listing services can help reach a larger audience and generate more leads.

Host open houses: Open houses are a great way to showcase a property and attract potential buyers. Hosting regular open houses can help generate interest and increase the visibility of the property.

Offer incentives: Offering incentives such as home warranties, closing cost assistance, or other bonuses can help attract potential buyers and close a sale. These incentives can help differentiate a property from others on the market and make it more appealing to potential buyers.

Work with a real estate agent: Working with a real estate agent can be beneficial when marketing and selling a property. Agents have access to a network of potential buyers, and can provide valuable advice on pricing, marketing, and negotiation.

By following these key steps and utilizing the right tools, investors can effectively market and sell their properties and generate a successful return on their investment.

Marketing a property can be a challenging task, but there are several proven strategies that can help increase its visibility and attract potential buyers. One of the most effective marketing strategies is to make use of real estate websites, such as Zillow, Redfin, and Realtor.com. These websites provide a platform for real estate professionals and property owners to showcase their properties, and they are visited by millions of potential buyers every day.

Another effective marketing strategy is to use social media platforms, such as Facebook, Instagram, and Twitter, to promote the property. This can be done by posting images and videos of the property, and sharing information about its features and location. Additionally, you can use paid advertising options on these platforms to reach a larger audience and target specific demographics.

Open house events can also be a valuable tool for marketing and selling properties. During an open house, potential buyers can tour the property, ask questions, and get a feel for its layout and features. Hosting open houses can help generate interest and create a buzz about the property, which can help increase its value and attract more potential buyers.

Using professional photography and video tours is another effective marketing strategy. High-quality images and videos can help showcase the property in its best light, and they can provide potential buyers with a virtual tour of the property, even if they are unable to physically visit the property. This can be especially helpful for buyers who are located far away or who are unable to visit the property in person.

Finally, working with a real estate agent can be one of the most effective strategies for marketing and selling properties. A good real estate agent will have a deep understanding of the local real estate market, and they will be able to use their network and expertise to connect potential buyers with the right properties. They can also provide valuable advice and guidance on how to price and market the property, and they can help negotiate the sale and handle all of the necessary paperwork and details.

Marketing a property effectively is crucial for its success in being sold. There are various marketing strategies that a real estate professional can use to make sure that the property is seen by potential buyers. Some of the popular marketing strategies include:

Online Listing: Posting the property on various online platforms, such as real estate websites, social media, and real estate apps can help reach a wider audience. This can help create a sense of urgency and drive interest in the property.

Virtual Tours: Creating a virtual tour of the property can be a great way to showcase the property's features and give potential buyers a feel for the layout and design. This can help create a sense of connection to the property and make it more appealing to potential buyers.

Brochures and Flyers: Creating high-quality brochures and flyers can be a great way to showcase the property's features and provide potential buyers with important information about the property, such as location, floor plan, and other important details.

Open Houses: Hosting open houses can be a great way to showcase the property and create a sense of urgency for potential buyers. This can also be a great opportunity for real estate professionals to meet potential buyers and answer any questions they may have.

The House Flipping Process: A Step-by-Step Guide to Wealth

Professional Photography: High-quality photos of the property can be a great way to showcase its features and make it more appealing to potential buyers. A professional photographer can help capture the property's best features and create an attractive visual representation of the property.

Referral Network: Building a referral network and leveraging it can be a great way to generate leads and find potential buyers. This can include referrals from past clients, family, and friends, as well as real estate agents and brokers.

Marketing a property effectively requires a comprehensive approach that utilizes a variety of strategies and techniques. By leveraging the right marketing tools and strategies, real estate professionals can help increase the visibility of the property, generate interest among potential buyers, and ultimately sell the property.

Marketing and selling properties effectively can make all the difference in the success of a real estate project. A well-planned marketing strategy will increase the visibility of the property, reach a wider audience and help in attracting potential buyers. Here are some tips for effective property marketing:

Utilize online platforms: Take advantage of online marketing platforms like real estate websites, social media, and online advertising to reach a wider audience. These platforms can provide detailed information on the property, location and price, making it easier for potential buyers to access and evaluate.

High-quality images and videos: Invest in high-quality images and videos of the property to showcase it in the best possible light. These visuals should accurately depict the property and its features, as well as the surrounding area.

Professional brochures: A well-designed brochure can be an effective marketing tool for properties. It should include information about the property, its features and benefits, location, and price. Brochures can be distributed through various channels, including real estate agencies, open house events, and mailings.

Open house events: Hosting an open house event can be an effective way to showcase the property and allow potential buyers to experience it in person. These events can provide an opportunity to interact with potential buyers, answer questions, and build relationships.

Effective pricing: Pricing a property accurately is crucial to attracting potential buyers and making a successful sale. Consider market trends, location, and the property's features and condition when determining an asking price.

In addition to marketing the property, it is also important to have a strong sales strategy in place. A well-executed sales plan will help close deals more efficiently and effectively. Here are some tips for successful property sales:

Qualify potential buyers: It is important to determine a buyer's financial ability and level of interest before engaging in negotiations. This can be done through pre-qualification processes, credit checks, and asking relevant questions.

Build relationships: Building a relationship with potential buyers can increase their level of trust and help in closing the deal. This can be done through regular communication, providing relevant information and addressing any concerns or questions they may have.

Negotiating skills: Effective negotiation skills are crucial in real estate sales. This involves understanding the buyer's needs, willingness to compromise and finding common ground for a successful sale.

Closing the deal: Once a sale has been agreed upon, it is important to close the deal efficiently and effectively. This can be done through the use of a sales agreement, closing documents, and conducting a thorough walk-through of the property to ensure it meets the buyer's expectations.

In conclusion, marketing and selling properties effectively is key to success in the real estate industry. A well-planned marketing strategy and strong sales plan can help reach a wider audience, attract potential buyers, and close deals efficiently and effectively.

Marketing and selling properties require a combination of effective strategies and strong communication skills. Real estate agents play a crucial role in the process of marketing and selling properties, as they help connect buyers and sellers, negotiate deals and close transactions.

One of the most important steps in marketing a property is to determine its target audience. This will help you tailor your marketing efforts towards the specific group of people who are most likely to be interested in the property. For example, if you're marketing a luxury apartment in a city center, you might target young professionals and urban dwellers.

Once you've identified your target audience, you'll want to create a marketing plan that is tailored to their specific needs and preferences. This could include using a variety of mediums to reach your audience, such as online listings, social media, direct mail campaigns, and open houses.

Another key aspect of marketing a property is presenting it in the best possible light. This means taking high-quality photos and videos, creating detailed descriptions of the property's features, and highlighting any unique selling points. You should also stage the property to make it look as inviting and appealing as possible.

Finally, it's important to price your property competitively. You should conduct a comparative market analysis to determine what similar properties in the area have sold for and price your property accordingly. Be sure to also consider factors such as the current market conditions and any local economic factors that could impact the price.

In conclusion, marketing and selling properties requires a combination of effective strategies, strong communication skills, and a deep understanding of your target audience. By following these tips, you can increase your chances of successfully marketing and selling your property.

Marketing and selling properties can be challenging, but it is an important part of the real estate industry. There are several strategies and techniques that can be used to market and sell properties effectively. The following are some key steps to consider when marketing and selling properties:

Determine the target market: The first step in marketing and selling properties is to determine the target market. This means identifying the type of buyer who is most likely to be interested in the property. For example, if the property is a family home, the target market is likely to be families with children. If the property is a luxury condo, the target market may be affluent professionals. Understanding the target market can help you tailor your marketing efforts to reach the right people.

Price the property correctly: Pricing the property correctly is critical to its success in the market. If the price is too high, potential buyers may be deterred, while if the price is too low, you may miss out on potential profits. A real estate agent can help you determine the right price for the property by analyzing comparable properties in the area.

Prepare the property for sale: Once you have determined the target market and priced the property correctly, it is time to prepare the property for sale. This may include cleaning, painting, and making any necessary repairs. You may also want to stage the property to help potential buyers visualize how they would use the space.

Create a marketing plan: The next step is to create a marketing plan. This should include a combination of online and offline marketing efforts. Online marketing can include creating a website, listing the property on real estate websites, and utilizing social media. Offline marketing can include open houses, newspaper and magazine ads, and direct mail campaigns.

Show the property: Showing the property is an important part of the marketing and selling process. This may involve hosting open houses, giving private tours, or both. It is important to have a clear and consistent showing process, as well as having the property in top condition when potential buyers visit.

Negotiate offers: When potential buyers make offers on the property, it is important to negotiate with them to reach a mutually acceptable agreement. A real estate agent can help you with this process by offering advice on how to respond to offers and by handling the negotiations on your behalf.

Close the sale: Once an offer has been accepted, it is time to close the sale. This involves completing all necessary paperwork, transferring the title, and making sure all financial arrangements have been made. A real estate attorney can help you with this process to ensure that everything is done correctly.

In conclusion, marketing and selling properties can be a complex and challenging process, but it can also be very rewarding. By following these steps, you can increase your chances of success and make the process as smooth and stress-free as possible.

Marketing and selling properties require a combination of creativity, effective communication, and understanding of the real estate market. One important aspect of marketing is creating an appealing listing. The listing should provide detailed information about the property, including its features, location, and any updates or renovations made. High-quality photos and virtual tours can also be used to showcase the property and provide a sense of what it would be like to live there.

Another important aspect of marketing is targeting the right audience. This can be done through online advertising, open houses, and word of mouth. Realtors can also use social media platforms like Facebook, Instagram, and LinkedIn to reach potential buyers and showcase their listings.

Effective communication is also key in marketing and selling properties. Realtors should be able to clearly and concisely explain the property's features and benefits to potential buyers. They should also be able to negotiate effectively and handle objections to close the sale.

When it comes to pricing, realtors must have a good understanding of the real estate market and comparable properties in the area. They should work with the seller to determine a fair and competitive price that will attract potential buyers.

Finally, it's important to build relationships with clients, both buyers and sellers. Realtors should make themselves available to answer questions and provide guidance throughout the buying or selling process. By offering excellent customer service, realtors can establish a strong reputation and generate repeat business.

Marketing a property effectively is essential to attracting potential buyers and securing a successful sale. Here are a few tips for marketing properties:

Utilize Online Listings: Online listings like Zillow, Redfin, and Realtor.com are a great way to reach a large audience. Make sure the property is listed with detailed information and high-quality images.

Utilize Social Media: Social media platforms like Facebook, Instagram, and LinkedIn are great ways to reach a target audience and generate interest in the property.

Host Open Houses: Open houses are a great way to showcase the property and generate interest. Make sure the property is clean, well-lit, and properly staged to create a positive impression.

Offer Incentives: Consider offering incentives like a closing cost credit or a home warranty to entice buyers.

Utilize Professional Photos: Professional photos can make a huge impact in attracting potential buyers. Make sure the photos highlight the best features of the property and show it in its best light.

The House Flipping Process: A Step-by-Step Guide to Wealth

Partner with Local Realtors: Consider partnering with local real estate agents to help market and sell the property. Real estate agents have access to a large network of potential buyers and can provide valuable insight into local market conditions.

In addition to these tips, it's important to have a clear understanding of the local real estate market and to price the property competitively. A well-marketed and priced property is more likely to attract interest and secure a successful sale.

Once you have completed all the necessary renovations and repairs, it's time to market and sell the property.

The first step in marketing and selling a property is to price it correctly. You can start by researching comparable properties in the area to see what they are selling for. Keep in mind the condition of the comparable properties and any upgrades or renovations you have made to your property. Price your property competitively, but not so low that you leave money on the table.

Next, it's time to showcase your property. High-quality photos and virtual tours are a must in today's real estate market. Make sure to highlight the key selling points of your property, such as natural light, spacious rooms, and updated finishes.

Another way to market your property is by hosting open houses. Open houses allow potential buyers to walk through the property, ask questions, and get a feel for the space. This can be a great way to generate interest and get offers on your property.

In addition to in-person marketing efforts, consider advertising your property online. Online listings can reach a large audience and can be a cost-effective way to market your property. Be sure to include detailed descriptions and plenty of high-quality photos to showcase your property.

It's also important to have a plan in place for handling offers. Be prepared to negotiate with buyers and make sure you understand the terms and conditions of any offers before accepting them.

Finally, make sure to work with a reputable real estate agent. An experienced real estate agent can help you navigate the marketing and selling process and can help you negotiate the best deal for your property.

In real estate marketing and selling, there are a variety of channels and tactics to reach potential buyers. Here are a few of the most common ones:

Online listing platforms: Online real estate marketplaces, such as Zillow and Redfin, offer a way for property owners to list their properties for sale and reach a large pool of potential buyers.

Social media: Social media platforms, such as Facebook and Instagram, can be used to reach potential buyers through paid advertising, or by showcasing properties through visual content such as photographs and videos.

Real estate agents: Real estate agents have a deep understanding of local markets and have access to a wide network of potential buyers. They can be hired to represent a property owner in the sale of a property.

Open houses: Holding open houses is a common way for sellers to showcase their property to potential buyers. This is an opportunity for buyers to view the property in person, ask questions and get a feel for the property.

Direct mail: Direct mail is a traditional marketing channel where property owners can send informational materials and advertisements to potential buyers. This can include property flyers, brochures, and postcards.

Brochures and property descriptions: A well-designed brochure or property description can be a useful tool for showcasing a property's features and benefits to potential buyers. It is important to highlight the unique selling points of the property and provide clear and concise information.

Virtual tours: Virtual tours allow potential buyers to tour a property from the comfort of their own home. This is especially useful for properties located in remote locations or for buyers who may not have the time to physically view a property.

In conclusion, there are many channels and tactics to reach potential buyers when marketing and selling properties. Choosing the right combination of strategies will depend on the target audience, the type of property, and the desired outcome.

In conclusion, marketing and selling properties requires a well thought out plan and strategy. From determining the target audience, to showcasing the property in its best light, to negotiating deals, it's important to have a thorough understanding of the market and the needs of potential buyers. By combining effective marketing techniques and excellent customer service, you can successfully sell properties and build a reputation as a trusted real estate professional. In order to stay ahead of the competition, it's important to constantly educate yourself on industry trends and best practices, and to stay abreast of changes in the real estate market. With careful planning, strong negotiation skills, and a commitment to providing exceptional customer service, you can achieve success in the competitive world of property sales.

"Success in real estate begins with a winning strategy, and the key to that strategy is marketing."

Chapter 6

Building a House Flipping Business

Building a house flipping business involves a series of steps and processes that can help you achieve success in this industry. Whether you are a seasoned real estate investor or a newcomer, you need to understand the basics of how this business works, as well as the essential elements that will help you build a strong foundation for your business.

The first step in building a house flipping business is to develop a business plan. This plan should outline your goals, strategies, and budget for your flipping business. You need to determine your target market, as well as the types of properties that you want to invest in. You should also identify your target demographics, such as first-time homebuyers, families, or retirees.

Once you have developed your business plan, you need to obtain financing for your business. You can obtain a loan from a bank, a private lender, or through crowdfunding. You should consider the interest rate, loan terms, and other loan features when selecting the best financing option for your business.

The next step in building a house flipping business is to find and evaluate properties. You can find properties through real estate listings, auction sites, or through your network of real estate agents and investors. Once you have found a potential property, you need to evaluate it to determine its potential for renovation and resale. This evaluation should include an assessment of the property's location, condition, and market value.

When you have found a property that you want to invest in, you need to renovate it to increase its value. You should hire a team of professionals, such as contractors, designers, and inspectors, to help you with the renovation process. You should also plan your renovation project carefully and budget for it appropriately, so you don't run into any financial difficulties during the renovation process.

Once the renovation is complete, you need to market and sell the property. You can list the property on real estate websites, or you can work with a real estate agent to sell the property. You should also develop a marketing strategy that will help you promote your property and attract potential buyers. You should also consider the pricing of your property, as well as the financing options that you will offer to buyers.

In conclusion, building a house flipping business requires a combination of planning, financing, and execution. You need to be patient, persistent, and focused on your goals, and you should always strive to improve your skills and knowledge in the real estate industry. With hard work, dedication, and a little bit of luck, you can build a successful house flipping business that will help you achieve your financial goals and dreams.

Building a successful house flipping business takes careful planning, dedication, and hard work. There are several key steps to building a profitable business in this industry:

Establish a solid business plan: The foundation of any successful business is a well-thought-out plan that outlines your goals, strategies, and steps for achieving them. Your business plan should include a marketing plan, financial projections, and a detailed timeline for each project.

Build a network: Networking is essential in this business, as you will need to build relationships with contractors, real estate agents, and other professionals in the industry. Attend industry events, join local real estate groups, and connect with others in the field to build your network and make valuable contacts.

Develop a strong brand: Your brand is your reputation and sets you apart from your competitors. It should be consistent across all marketing materials, from your website and business cards to your social media profiles and advertisements.

Get financing: To be successful in the flipping business, you need access to capital. You may choose to secure financing through a traditional bank loan, hard money lender, or private investor. Consider your options and choose the best option that meets your needs and goals.

Learn the real estate market: It's important to stay informed about the real estate market, including market trends, property values, and zoning regulations. This information will help you make informed decisions about which properties to invest in and how to best renovate them for maximum return on investment.

Build a team: As your business grows, you may need to hire additional help, including contractors, real estate agents, and administrative staff. Choose your team members carefully and make sure they share your values and commitment to quality.

Set realistic goals: It's important to set realistic goals and expectations for your business. Focus on steady growth and profitability, and don't take on more than you can handle. Remember, success takes time and hard work.

By following these steps and remaining dedicated to your business, you can build a successful house flipping business that is profitable and sustainable over the long term.

Building a successful house flipping business requires careful planning, organization, and execution. Here are some key elements to consider as you lay the foundation for your business:

Business Structure: Choose the right legal structure for your business, such as sole proprietorship, partnership, limited liability company (LLC), or corporation. Each structure has its own set of legal, tax, and liability implications, so it's important to understand the pros and cons of each before making a decision.

Financing: Secure financing for your business through traditional banks, private lenders, or hard money lenders. This can include a combination of personal savings, credit cards, home equity loans, and other types of financing.

Marketing and Branding: Develop a strong brand identity for your business, including a logo, business cards, and website. Market your business through targeted advertising campaigns, networking events, and social media platforms.

Contractors and Suppliers: Build a network of trusted contractors, suppliers, and vendors to help with the renovation and flipping process. This can include general contractors, plumbers, electricians, roofers, painters, and more.

Systems and Processes: Create systems and processes for your business to ensure a smooth and efficient workflow. This can include standard operating procedures for buying, renovating, and selling properties, as well as record-keeping, budgeting, and tracking systems.

Legal and Compliance: Stay compliant with all applicable laws and regulations, including real estate, tax, and labor laws. Hire an attorney and accountant to help with legal and financial matters.

Network and Mentors: Build a network of fellow real estate investors and seek the advice of experienced professionals in the industry. Join real estate investment groups and attend events and workshops to learn from other investors.

By following these steps and continuously seeking opportunities for growth and improvement, you can build a successful and sustainable house flipping business.

When building a house flipping business, it is important to have a clear and well-defined plan. This plan should outline the steps you will take to find, purchase, renovate, and sell properties. It should also include a timeline for each step and an estimate of the costs involved.

Having a plan in place will help ensure that your business runs smoothly and reduces the chances of encountering unexpected problems along the way. It also helps you stay focused and avoid making costly mistakes. A well-written plan will also help you secure financing and attract potential investors.

In addition to having a plan, it is important to have a clear understanding of the market you are operating in. Research the local real estate market, including the average home prices, rental rates, and demand for rental properties. This will give you a better understanding of the potential profits and risks involved in the market.

Another important aspect of building a successful house flipping business is building a strong team. This includes finding reliable contractors, real estate agents, and other professionals who can help you throughout the process. It is also important to have a good understanding of the local building codes and regulations, as well as the financial and legal aspects of buying and selling properties.

To help you build a successful house flipping business, consider taking courses and attending seminars on real estate investing and property management. This will give you a deeper understanding of the industry and help you stay up-to-date on the latest trends and best practices.

In conclusion, building a successful house flipping business requires careful planning, research, and attention to detail. It also requires a strong commitment to the business, a willingness to learn and grow, and a passion for real estate. With these attributes, you can build a successful and profitable house flipping business.

Building a house flipping business requires careful planning, strategy, and execution. The following are important steps to consider when starting a house flipping business:

Conduct Market Research: Analyze the local real estate market to understand the current demand for properties, median prices, and what types of properties are selling. This will help you determine the best areas to invest in and what properties are likely to be profitable.

Create a Business Plan: Outline your goals, target market, marketing strategies, budget, and expected returns. This will help you stay focused and organized as you grow your business.

Build a Strong Network: Network with real estate agents, contractors, and other professionals in the industry to gain insight into the local market and get leads on potential properties.

Secure Funding: Determine the best funding options for your business, whether it be private investors, loans, or a combination of both. Make sure you have enough capital to purchase properties and cover any renovation costs.

Acquire Properties: Start buying properties that fit your investment criteria and begin the renovation process.

Renovate Properties: Work with a team of professionals to complete necessary renovations and updates to the properties. This includes contractors, architects, and designers.

Market and Sell Properties: Develop a marketing plan to effectively showcase the properties you have renovated. This can include online advertising, open houses, and other promotional activities.

Track Progress and Evaluate Results: Continuously monitor the success of your business by tracking key metrics such as cost of renovations, time to sell, and profits. This will help you make informed decisions and improve your business strategies over time.

The House Flipping Process: A Step-by-Step Guide to Wealth

In conclusion, building a successful house flipping business requires careful planning, strategy, and execution. By following these steps and continuously tracking and evaluating your results, you can achieve success in the real estate industry.

Building a house flipping business requires more than just buying, renovating, and selling properties. It requires careful planning, a solid understanding of the market, and a well-defined business plan. Here are some examples of how to build a successful house flipping business:

Establish clear goals and objectives: Determine what type of properties you want to flip, your target market, and your desired profit margins. This will help you make informed decisions about which properties to pursue and what renovations to make.

Build a team: As your business grows, it's important to have a team of professionals to help you with various aspects of the process. This may include a real estate agent, contractor, accountant, and attorney.

Create a budget: House flipping can be expensive, so it's important to have a clear understanding of your financial resources and to create a budget for each project. This will help you avoid overspending and ensure that you have enough money to complete the renovation and sell the property for a profit.

Network with other flippers and investors: Building a network of other flippers and investors can provide valuable insights, advice, and even potential business opportunities. Attend real estate events, join local investment groups, and connect with other flippers online to expand your network.

Develop a marketing plan: Effective marketing is key to attracting potential buyers and selling properties quickly. Develop a marketing plan that includes online advertising, social media, open houses, and other strategies to reach your target market.

Continuously educate yourself: The real estate market is constantly changing, so it's important to stay up-to-date on the latest trends and strategies. Attend seminars, read books, and follow industry leaders to continue to grow your knowledge and skills.

Building a successful house flipping business requires careful planning and execution. One key aspect is creating a clear business plan that outlines the steps you need to take to reach your goals. This should include a market analysis to identify the best opportunities for flipping properties, as well as a financial plan to ensure you have the resources you need to purchase and renovate properties.

Another important factor is building a strong network of professionals who can help you along the way. This might include real estate agents, contractors, and inspectors who can provide valuable insights and support as you navigate the process. Building relationships with these individuals can also help you stay up-to-date on market trends and opportunities, which can be key to success in this industry.

In addition to these key elements, it is also important to stay organized and focused as you build your business. This might mean using tools and systems to manage your finances, schedule your projects, and track your progress. For example, you may use a project management platform to keep track of the progress of your renovations, or a budgeting tool to monitor your expenses.

Finally, it's important to be willing to adapt and adjust your strategy as you go. The housing market is constantly evolving, and success in house flipping often requires the ability to quickly respond to changes in the market. This might mean being open to new opportunities, adjusting your approach to renovations, or modifying your marketing strategies to reach new audiences. By staying nimble and open-minded, you can help ensure the success of your business over the long term.

Building a successful house flipping business requires careful planning and execution. In addition to finding and purchasing properties to renovate, there are several key steps involved in setting up and running a profitable business.

First, it is important to create a solid business plan that outlines your goals, target market, and financial projections. This plan should also include a marketing strategy for finding potential properties, as well as a budget for renovations and overhead costs.

Next, you should consider the type of company structure you would like to establish, such as a sole proprietorship, partnership, or limited liability company (LLC). This decision will impact your personal liability, taxes, and overall financial management.

It is also important to establish a network of trusted professionals, such as real estate agents, contractors, and accountants. These individuals can provide valuable support and expertise as you build your business.

In addition to securing financing for your properties, it is important to have a system in place for managing renovations, such as setting a budget, scheduling work, and monitoring progress. This may include hiring a project manager or utilizing project management software.

Finally, it is important to stay up-to-date on industry trends and regulations, such as zoning laws, building codes, and environmental standards. This can help you stay compliant and make informed decisions as you grow your business.

Example:
John has always been interested in real estate and has decided to start a house flipping business. He starts by creating a detailed business plan that outlines his goals, target market, and budget for renovations and overhead costs. He also establishes a LLC for his business and hires a real estate agent to help him find potential properties. He secures financing for his first few renovations and sets up a system for managing the projects, including hiring a project manager to oversee the work. As he grows his business,

John continues to stay informed on industry trends and regulations to ensure the success of his business.

Building a successful house flipping business requires more than just buying and selling properties. It requires a well thought out strategy, careful planning, and the ability to execute on your plans.

One important aspect of building a house flipping business is to establish clear goals and objectives. This could include things like targeting specific neighborhoods, setting a budget for each project, and determining how many properties you want to flip per year. Having clear goals and objectives will help guide your decisions and keep you on track.

Another important aspect is building a team. This could include contractors, real estate agents, and other professionals who can help you with the buying and selling process. You'll also want to build a network of trusted individuals who can provide you with leads on potential properties, help with financing, and provide you with support and advice.

Another key aspect of building a house flipping business is to have a solid understanding of the real estate market and the neighborhoods where you plan to work. This includes knowing what properties are selling for, what the demand for rental properties is, and what the economic trends are in the area. You can research this information online, attend real estate conferences, or work with a real estate agent who specializes in the area you're interested in.

Finally, it's important to have a plan for financing your projects. This could include getting a loan from a bank, using private investors, or partnering with a silent partner. Whichever option you choose, be sure to carefully consider the terms and conditions of the financing, and make sure it aligns with your goals and objectives.

For example, if you are looking to flip multiple properties in a short period of time, a loan from a bank may not be the best option. Instead, you might consider working with private investors who are willing to provide you with the capital you need in exchange for a share of the profits. This approach allows you to raise the capital you need quickly, and you don't have to worry about paying back the loan over an extended period of time.

To build a successful house flipping business, it is important to have a solid business plan in place. This plan should include a clear mission statement, financial projections, and a marketing strategy. A well-defined business plan will provide a roadmap for success and help ensure that all stakeholders are on the same page. It is also important to have a strong network of professionals, including contractors, real estate agents, and financial advisors. These individuals can provide valuable guidance and support throughout the flipping process. Additionally, it is important to continually educate yourself about the latest industry trends and regulations to stay ahead of the competition. This can be done through attending industry events, reading industry publications, and participating in continuing education courses. By building strong relationships and staying informed, you can build a thriving house flipping business.

In conclusion, building a successful house flipping business requires a strategic approach, planning, and hard work. It involves sourcing for properties, securing financing, renovating properties, marketing, and selling them. To be successful, it is important to understand the real estate market, develop a business plan, and build a reliable network of professionals to help you in various aspects of the business.
Additionally, staying organized and keeping accurate records will help you to keep track of your expenses, profits, and overall business performance. With persistence, dedication, and an eye for detail, anyone can build a thriving house flipping business.

"The future of your house flipping business lies in your hands. Build it with care and it will stand the test of time."

THE END

The end of this book marks the beginning of your journey to building a successful house flipping business. You have learned the importance of creating a comprehensive business plan, conducting thorough property research, developing effective marketing and sales strategies, and managing your finances and renovation projects effectively. These tips and techniques, combined with your determination and hard work, will help you achieve your goals and create a profitable business. Always remember to keep learning and growing, stay focused on your goals, and stay true to your values and principles. With these qualities, you will be well on your way to success.

If you learned something valuable from this book, please rate us on Amazon. If you would like to learn more on creating Rental Income from Real Estate Investing, do checkout our book -

RENT TO WEALTH: The Proven Path to Financial Freedom through Rental Property (Real Estate Investing)

It's available on Amazon in Paperback, Hardcover and Kindle format.

We wish you all the best for your House Flipping business and you shall achieve all the success in your life.

: A Step-by-Step Guide to Wealth
The House Flipping Process: A Step-by-Step Guide to Wealth

The House Flipping Process: A Step-by-Step Guide to Wealth

www.ingramcontent.com/pod-product-compliance
Lightning Source LLC
Chambersburg PA
CBHW031421210526
45464CB00005B/1987